Janet Wright

EDINBURGH

THE MINI ROUGH GUIDE

KT-557-292

There are more than one hundred Rough
Guide travel, phrasebook, and music titles,
covering destinations from Amsterdam to
Zimbabwe, languages from Czech to Thai,
and musics from World to Opera and Jazz

Forthcoming titles include

Bangkok • Barbados • Japan
Jordan • Syria • Music USA
Country Music

Rough Guides on the Internet

http://www.roughguides.com

Rough Guide Credits

Text editor: Julia Kelly. Series editor: Mark Ellingham
Typesetting: Andy Hilliard, Judy Pang
Cartography: David Callier, Maxine Burke

Publishing Information

This first edition published February 1998 by
Rough Guides Ltd, 1 Mercer St, London WC2H 9QJ.

Distributed by the Penguin Group:
Penguin Books Ltd, 27 Wrights Lane, London W8 5TZ
Penguin Books USA Inc., 375 Hudson Street, New York 10014, USA
Penguin Books Australia Ltd, 487 Maroondah Highway,
PO Box 257, Ringwood, Victoria 3134, Australia
Penguin Books Canada Ltd, 10 Alcorn Avenue,
Toronto, Ontario, Canada M4V 1E4
Penguin Books (NZ) Ltd, 182–190 Wairau Road,
Auckland 10, New Zealand

Typeset in Bembo and Helvetica to an original design by Henry Iles.
Printed in Spain by Graphy Cems.

© The Rough Guides Ltd 1998. 224pp, includes index
A catalogue record for this book is available from the British Library.
ISBN 1-85828-295-0

EDINBURGH

THE MINI ROUGH GUIDE

by Julian Ward
and Gordon McLachlan

We set out to do something different when the first Rough Guide was published in 1982. Mark Ellingham, just out of university, was travelling in Greece. He brought along the popular guides of the day, but found they were all lacking in some way. They were either strong on ruins and museums but went on for pages without mentioning a beach or taverna. Or they were so conscious of the need to save money that they lost sight of Greece's cultural and historical significance. Also, none of the books told him anything about Greece's contemporary life – its politics, its culture, its people, and how they lived.

So with no job in prospect, Mark decided to write his own guidebook, one which aimed to provide practical information that was second to none, detailing the best beaches and the hottest clubs and restaurants, while also giving hard-hitting accounts of every sight, both famous and obscure, and providing up-to-the-minute information on contemporary culture. It was a guide that encouraged independent travellers to find the best of Greece, and was a great success, getting shortlisted for the Thomas Cook travel guide award, and encouraging Mark, along with three friends, to expand the series.

The Rough Guide list grew rapidly and the letters flooded in, indicating a much broader readership than had been anticipated, but one which uniformly appreciated the Rough Guide mix of practical detail and humour, irreverence and enthusiasm. Things haven't changed. The same four friends who began the series are still the caretakers of the Rough Guide mission today: to provide the most reliable, up-to-date and entertaining information to independent-minded travellers of all ages, on all budgets.

We now publish more than 100 titles and have offices in London and New York. The travel guides are written and researched by a dedicated team of more than 100 authors, based in Britain, Europe, the USA and Australia. We have also created a unique series of phrasebooks to accompany the travel series, along with an acclaimed series of music guides, and a best-selling pocket guide to the Internet and World Wide Web. We also publish comprehensive travel information on our web site: **http://www.roughguides.com**

Help Us Update

We've gone to a lot of effort to ensure that this first edition of *The Rough Guide to Edinburgh* is as up to date and accurate as possible. However, if you feel there are places we've under-rated or over-praised, or find we've missed something good or covered something which has now gone, then please write: suggestions, comments or corrections are much appreciated.

We'll credit all contributions, and send a copy of the next edition (or any other Rough Guide if you prefer) for the best letters. Please mark letters: "Rough Guide Edinburgh Update" and send to:

Rough Guides, 1 Mercer St, London WC2H 9QJ, or
Rough Guides, 375 Hudson St, 9th floor, New York NY 10014.
Or send email to: mail@roughguides.co.uk

Online updates about this book can be found on
Rough Guides' Web site (see opposite)

The Authors

After living in London for several years and travelling extensively in Africa and Eastern Asia, **Julian Ward** moved to Edinburgh in 1986 to study Chinese. He recently completed a PhD on Xu Xiake, unknown in the West but regarded as China's foremost travel writer. He lives in Portobello with his family.

Gordon McLachlan was born and educated in Edinburgh, where he still lives. Over the past decade, in addition to this book, he has written the *Rough Guide to Germany*, contributed to the *Scotland*, *Britain* and *Poland* Rough Guides, and written books on Berlin and Southern Germany's Romantic Road.

Acknowledgements

Thanks to Kate Britee, Calum Colvin, Thom Dibdin, Marianne Dunbar, Ian Dunn, Jane Ferguson, Gordon McCulloch, Jenny Wilson, Mike Windle and the staff of the Scottish Library.

CONTENTS

Introduction   viii

The Guide   1

1   Introducing the city   3

2   Edinburgh Castle   9

3   The Royal Mile   18

4   Holyroodhouse to Craigmillar   37

5   Cowgate to the University   45

6   The New Town   55

7   The suburbs   76

8   Day-trips from Edinburgh   86

Listings   95

9   Accommodation   97

10 Eating   111

11 Drinking   139

12 Live music and clubs   149

13 Theatre, comedy and cinema   156

14 Art galleries   161

15	Gay Edinburgh	164
16	Kids' Edinburgh	168
17	Shopping	172
18	Festivals and events	182
19	Directory	190

Contexts		195
History		197
Film		204
Books		206
Index		209

INTRODUCTION

Perched on a series of extinct volcanoes and rocky crags which rise from the generally flat landscape of the Lothians, Edinburgh has a natural setting unrivalled by any other major European city. One native author of genius, Robert Louis Stevenson, best captured the feel of his "precipitous city" and the key role of its site, declaring that "No situation could be more commanding for the head of a kingdom; none better chosen for noble prospects".

The Old Town and New Town, which between them contain most of the main sights, form a fascinatingly contrasted pair, the former tightly packed, brooding and still predominantly medieval, the latter a planning masterpiece of the Age of Enlightenment, when Edinburgh provided the European lead in many fields of intellectual endeavour. Only about half of the total area of the city is built up, and it has a marvellous range of parks as well as a seemingly inexhaustible supply of surprising and dramatic vistas. From the towering fairytale Castle to the royal palace of Holyroodhouse, the Old Town preserves all the key reminders of its role as a capital, while, in contrast, a tantalizing glimpse of the wild beauty of Scotland's scenery can be had immediately beyond the palace in Holyrood Park.

Also within the municipal boundaries are rural villages such as Duddingston and Dalmeny; the old royal burgh of South Queensferry, with its spectacular pair of bridges spanning the Forth; the seaside resort of Portobello; and the port of Leith, which has revived from a long period in the doldrums to become a hip residential area and the new home of the Scottish Office.

Although the Scottish parliament wound itself up in 1707, Edinburgh never lost the style, appearance and trappings of a capital city and is well placed to resume its political role when the devolved parliament – whose creation was backed by a decisive vote in the 1997 referendum – is set up at the start of the new millennium.

An artistic phenomenon of long standing and proven worth is the Edinburgh International Festival, the world's largest such extravaganza, which is in reality a series of separate festivals catering to every conceivable audience. Around a million visitors flock to the city when it is held each August, generating a carnival atmosphere which is absent – save for the boisterous celebrations centred on Hogmanay – for the remaining eleven months of the calendar. Nonetheless, Edinburgh maintains a vibrant cultural life throughout the year. Among the city's many museums, the National Gallery of Scotland boasts as choice an array of Old Masters as can be found anywhere; its offshoot, the Scottish National Gallery of Modern Art, has Britain's oldest specialist collection of twentieth-century painting and sculpture.

The city also has a superb range of restaurants offering most leading international cuisines as well as a wide variety of theatres and music venues. Its distinctive *howffs* (pubs), allied to its brewing and distilling traditions, have given it the status of a great drinking city and the presence of three universities, plus several colleges, means that there is a youthful presence for most of the year – a welcome corrective to the stuffiness which is often regarded as Edinburgh's Achilles heel.

Climate

Edinburgh's strong winds and heavy rain make warm clothes and sturdy umbrellas a must at any time of the year. Even after a few warm days in high summer, a *haar* or sea mist is wont to roll in from the Firth of Forth and envelop the city. The coldest months are January and February when the highest daily temperature averages at 6°C (42° F) and the lowest just 1°C (34°F). July is the warmest month, reaching an average high of 18°C (65°F).

	°F Average daily		°C Average daily		Rainfall Average monthly	
	max	min	max	min	in	mm
Jan	42	34	6	1	2.2	57
Feb	43	34	6	1	1.5	39
March	46	36	8	2	1.5	39
April	51	39	11	4	1.5	39
May	56	43	14	6	2.1	54
June	62	49	17	9	1.9	47
July	65	52	18	11	3.3	83
Aug	64	52	18	11	3.0	77
Sept	60	49	16	9	2.2	57
Oct	54	44	12	7	2.6	65
Nov	48	39	9	4	2.4	62
Dec	44	36	7	2	2.2	57

THE GUIDE

1	Introducing the city	3
2	Edinburgh Castle	9
3	The Royal Mile	18
4	Holyroodhouse to Craigmillar	37
5	Cowgate to the University	45
6	The New Town	55
7	The suburbs	76
8	Day-trips from Edinburgh	86

INTRODUCING THE CITY

Edinburgh occupies a large area relative to its population, which numbers less than half a million. Nonetheless, the majority of its attractions lie in the city centre, which is readily explored on foot. The **Old Town**, which occupies a narrow crag, preserves all the key reminders of the city's historic role as Scotland's capital. At the highest point is **Edinburgh Castle**, home of the spectacular crown jewels, the Honours of Scotland, while at the lowest point is the **Palace of Holyroodhouse**, which maintains its historic function as the monarch's Scottish residence. Along the **Royal Mile** which links them are the hammerbeamed **Parliament Hall** and the crown-spired **St Giles**, the nearest there is to a principal church in the Scots Kirk's rigorously egalitarian framework. The tortuous wynds and tightly packed closes of the Old Town are also strongly associated with Edinburgh's underworld lore, and in particular with the schizophrenic Deacon Brodie, the direct inspiration for Stevenson's *Dr Jekyll & Mr Hyde*, and the body snatchers Burke and Hare. South of the Royal

Mile, the district loses its medieval character; here can be found such fine buildings as the **University**, a late masterpiece of Robert Adam, and the splendid Venetian-style *palazzo* that houses the **Royal Museum of Scotland**.

The main thoroughfare of the **New Town**, **Princes Street**, offers wonderful views of the Old Town skyline, while unexpected vistas of the Firth of Forth open out from the elevated streets to the north. There are many magnificent Neoclassical set pieces here, notably Adam's **Register House** and **Charlotte Square**, Thomas Hamilton's **Old Royal High School** – for a long time earmarked as the home of the new Scottish Parliament – and William Henry Playfair's **Royal Scottish Academy** and **National Gallery of Scotland**. The last of these houses as fine an array of paintings as you could ever expect to find, and has two outstations elsewhere in the New Town in the **Scottish National Portrait Gallery** and the **Scottish National Gallery of Modern Art**, Britain's oldest specialist collection of twentieth-century painting and sculpture.

A tantalizing sample of the wild beauty of Scotland's scenery can be had in **Holyrood Park**, an extensive area of open countryside in the very heart of the city, which is dominated by the highest and most impressive of Edinburgh's volcanoes, **Arthur's Seat**. Very different in character are the manicured **Royal Botanic Garden** to the north of the New Town, and **Edinburgh Zoo**, which is set on a hillside in western part of the city.

Other major attractions in the outskirts include **Craigmillar Castle** and, to the east of the city, **Tantallon Castle**, positioned dramatically on a headland surrounded on three sides by the Firth of Forth. Additionally, there are several other districts along the Firth of Forth with their own very distinct identity, among them the seaside resort of **Portobello** and the port of **Leith**.

The telephone code for Edinburgh is Ⓒ0131.
Calling Edinburgh from abroad, dial Ⓒ0044-131
followed by the subscriber's number.

Arrival

Edinburgh International Airport (Ⓒ333 1000) is at Turnhouse, seven miles west of the city centre, close to the start of the M8 motorway to Glasgow. There's a **tourist office** in its main concourse opposite Gate 5 (see below). Regular shuttle buses (£3.20) connect to Waverley Station in the town centre; taxis charge around £11 for the same journey.

Waverley Station (Ⓒ556 2451), at the eastern end of Princes Street, is the terminus for all mainline **trains**. All lines west and north are also served by Haymarket Station at the junction of Dalry Road and Haymarket Terrace in the west end of the city.

The main **bus terminal** is located on St Andrew Square, a few minutes' walk from Waverley Station. One of the major bus companies, SMT (Scottish Midland Transport), has a shop at the southeastern corner of the station (Mon–Fri 8.40am–5pm, Sat 9am–5pm; Ⓒ558 1616).

Information

Edinburgh's main **tourist office**, which is well run and offers vast amounts of information, is at 3 Princes St (April & Oct Mon–Sat 9am–6pm, Sun 10am–6pm; May, June & Sept Mon–Sat 9am–7pm, Sun 10am–7pm; July & Aug Mon–Sat 9am–8pm, Sun 10am–8pm; Nov–March Mon–Sat 9am–6pm, Sun 10am–8pm; Ⓒ557 1700). Services provided include **accommodation** reservations (Ⓒ557

9755) and money exchange. You can also pick up various publications here: one you shouldn't do without is the excellent fortnightly **listings** magazine, *The List*, which provides coverage of the arts in Edinburgh as well as comprehensive listings of forthcoming events. There's a much smaller **airport branch** of the tourist office (April–Oct Mon–Sat 8.30am–9.30pm, Sun 9.30am–9.30pm; Nov–March Mon–Fri 9am–6pm, Sat 9am–5pm, Sun 9.30am–5pm; ✆333 2167).

Transport

Edinburgh is well-served by **buses**, although even locals are confused by the consequences of deregulation, with several companies offering competing services along similar routes.

Most useful are the maroon buses operated by Lothian Regional Transport (LRT); all buses referred to in the text are run by them unless otherwise stated. Timetables and **passes** are available from most newsagents and at the ticket centres at 31 Waverley Bridge (May–Oct Mon–Sat 8am–7.15pm, Sun 9.00am–4.30pm; Nov–April Mon–Fri 9am–4.30pm; ✆225 8616) or 27 Hanover St (Mon–Sat 8.30am–6.00pm; ✆554 4494). A standard fare for short journeys is 85p but a good investment, especially if you're staying far out or want to explore the suburbs, is the £10 pass allowing a week's unlimited travel on LRT buses (passport photo needed). You can also buy an LRT day-pass for £2.20, or tickets from the driver, for which you'll need exact change.

The green buses run by Eastern Scottish, and the green and yellow buses of Lowland Scottish, link the capital with outlying towns and villages. Most services depart from and terminate at the St Andrew Square bus station. For longer journeys, there is a large National Express booking office in the station: for journeys within Scotland, ring ℗0990 505050; for cross-border travel, ring ℗0990 808080.

SIGHTSEEING TOURS

Of the guided tours available, the best are the Guide Friday (℗556 2244) open-topped buses, which depart from Waverley Station and cruise through the city streets, allowing you to get on and off at leisure. Alternatively, take a walking tour with Mercat Tours (℗661 4541), 47 Willowbrae Avenue, which range from strolls along the Royal Mile (daily: April–Sept 2pm & 11pm; Oct–March 2pm) to evening "Ghost and Ghoul" tours (daily: April–Sept 7pm & 8pm; Oct–March 8pm) and visits to the vaults beneath the South Bridge. For further information, check out the billboards by the Tron Kirk or the Mercat Cross beside St Giles Kirk, from where most Mercat tours leave. Other tours worth considering are the Audio Walking Tours, Tollbooth Church, Castlehill (daily 10am–8pm; ℗220 3030), covering over five hundred years of the city's history with headphones and a printed guide, and Witchery Tours at 352 Castlehill, Royal Mile (daily 10am–11pm; ℗225 6745), who organize costumed tours starting off from the *Witchery Restaurant*.

For a bird's-eye view of the city, Forth Helicopter Services, Edinburgh Airport (℗339 2321), organize fifteen-minute helicopter trips over the city and the Forth Bridge at a cost of £50 per person.

The city has plenty of taxi ranks, especially around Waverley Bridge, and it's also relatively easy to hail one on the street. Costs start at £1.20 for the first 340yd and 20p for each additional 240yd. The phone numbers of the main

TRANSPORT

local cab companies are: Capital Castle Cabs (℡228 2555), Central Radio Taxis (℡229 2468) and City Cabs (℡228 1211).

It is emphatically *not* a good idea to take a **car** into central Edinburgh: despite the presence of several expensive multi-storey car parks, looking for somewhere to park often involves long, fruitless searches. Most ticket and parking meter regulations are in force from 8.30am to 5.30pm Monday to Friday, and from 8.30am to 1.30pm on Saturday.

Edinburgh is a reasonably cycle-friendly city – although hilly – with several **cycle paths**. The local cycling action group, Spokes (℡313 2114), publishes an excellent cycle map of the city. For rental, try Central Cycles, 13 Lochrin Place (℡228 6333), Edinburgh Cycle Hire, 29 Blackfriars St (℡556 5560), or Sandy Gilchrist Cycles, 1 Cadzow Place (℡652 1760).

EDINBURGH CASTLE

The imposing bulk of **Edinburgh Castle** dominates the skyline of the entire city from atop its crag volcanic rock. It requires no great imaginative feat to comprehend the strategic importance that underpinned the castle's, and hence Edinburgh's, pre-eminence within Scotland: in the dramatic view from Princes Street, the north side rears high above an almost sheer rockface; the southern side is equally formidable, the western, where the rock rises in terraces, only marginally less so. Would-be attackers, like modern tourists, were forced to approach the castle from the crag to the east, along which the Royal Mile runs down to Holyrood.

The castle's disparate styles reflect its many changes in usage, as well as advances in military architecture: the oldest surviving part, St Margaret's Chapel, is from the twelfth century, while the most recent additions date back to the 1920s. Nothing remains from its period as a seat of the Scottish court in the reign of Malcolm III (the king who overthrew Macbeth in 1057). Indeed, having been lost to (and subsequently recaptured from) the English on several occasions, the defences were dismantled by the Scots themselves in 1313, and only rebuilt in 1356 when the return of King David II from captivity introduced a modicum of political stability. Thereafter, it gradually developed into Scotland's premier castle, with the dual function of fortress and royal palace. It last saw action in 1745, when the Young Pretender's forces, fresh from their victory at Prestonpans, made a half-hearted attempt to storm it. Subsequently, advances in weapon technology diminished its importance, but under the influence of the Romantic movement it came to be seen as a great national monument. A grandiose "improvement" scheme, which would have transformed it into a bloated nineteenth-century vision of the Middle Ages, was considered, but (perhaps fortunately) only a few elements of it were actually built.

....

Edinburgh Castle (map 5) is open daily: April–Sept 9.30am–6pm; Oct–March 9.30am–5pm; £5.50.

....

Though you can easily take in the views and wander round the castle yourself, you might like to join one of the somewhat overheated **guided tours** offered by kilted locals, furiously hamming up a thick Scottish brogue as they talk of war, boiling oil and the roar of the cannon.

The Esplanade

The castle is entered via the **Esplanade**, a parade ground laid out in the eighteenth century and enclosed a hundred years later by ornamental walls, the southern one of which commands fine views towards the Pentland Hills. Each evening during the Festival (see p.183), the Esplanade is the setting for the city's most shameless and spectacular demonstration of tourist kitsch, the Edinburgh Military Tattoo (see p.188). An unfortunate side effect of this is that the skyline is disfigured for virtually the entire summer by the grandstands needed to accommodate the spectators.

In the northeast corner are two reminders of unhappy times. An Art Nouveau **drinking fountain** of witches' heads entwined by a snake marks the spot where around three hundred women deemed to be witches were burned at the stake between 1479 and 1722, and nearby an equestrian **statue of Field Marshal Earl Haig** recalls the controversial Edinburgh-born commander of the British forces in World War I, whose trench warfare strategy of sending men "over the top" led to previously unimaginable casualties.

The lower defences

The **Gatehouse** to the castle is a Romantic-style addition of the 1880s, complete with the last drawbridge ever built in Scotland. It was later adorned with appropriately heroic-looking statues of Sir William Wallace and Robert the Bruce.

Continuing uphill, you pass through the **Portcullis Gate**, a handsome Renaissance gateway, marred by the addition of a nineteenth-century upper storey known as the **Argyle Tower**, which is equipped with anachronistic arrow slits. The tower was named after Archibald, ninth Earl of Argyll, who was said to have been imprisoned in a room above the Portcullis Gate prior to his execution in 1685.

Beyond is the six-gun **Argyle Battery**, built in the eighteenth century by Major General Wade, whose network of military roads and bridges still forms an essential part of the transport infrastructure of the Highlands. Further west on **Mill's Mount Battery**, a well-known Edinburgh ritual takes place – the daily firing of the 1pm gun. Originally designed for the benefit of ships in the Firth of Forth, it's now continued as a time signal by city-centre workers. Both batteries offer wonderful panoramic views over Princes Street and the New Town to the coastal towns and hills of Fife across the Forth.

Up the tortuously sloping road, the **Governor's House** is a 1740s mansion whose harled masonry and crow-stepped gables are archetypal features of vernacular Scottish architecture. It now serves as the officers' mess for members of the garrison, while the governor himself lives in the northern side wing. Behind stands the largest single construction in the castle complex, the **New Barracks**, built in the 1790s in an austere Neoclassical style. The road then snakes round towards the enclosed citadel at the uppermost point of Castle Rock, entered via **Foog's Gate**.

St Margaret's Chapel

At the eastern end of the citadel, **St Margaret's Chapel** is the oldest surviving building in the castle, and probably in Edinburgh itself. Used as a powder magazine for 300 years, this tiny Norman church was rediscovered in 1845 and was eventually rededicated in 1934, after sympathetic restoration. Externally it is plain and severe, but the interior preserves an elaborate zigzag archway dividing the nave from the sanctuary. Although once believed to have been built by the saint herself, and mooted as the site of her death in 1093, its architectural style suggests that it dates from about thirty years later, and was thus probably built by King David I as a memorial to his mother.

The battlements in front of the chapel offer the best of all the castle's panoramic views. They are interrupted by the **Lang Stairs**, which provide an alternative means of access from the Argyle Battery via the side of the Portcullis Gate. Just below the battlements there's a small **cemetery**, the last resting place of the soldiers' pets: it is kept in immaculate condition, particularly when contrasted with the dilapidated state of some of the city's public cemeteries. Continuing eastwards, you skirt the top of the Forewall and Half Moon Batteries, passing the 108-foot **Castle Well** en route to **Crown Square**, the highest, most secure and most important section of the entire complex. The Half Moon Battery stands on the site of David's Tower, which was the setting for the infamous **Black Dinner** in 1440, when the keeper of the castle, Sir William Crichton, effectively the guardian of the 9-year-old King James II, son of the murdered James I, arranged for a potential rival, the Earl of Douglas, and his younger brother to attend a meal in the tower. After a huge banquet, the visitors were presented with a bull's head (a sign of condemnation to death) accused of treason and summarily executed in the castle courtyard.

The Palace

The eastern side of Crown Square is occupied by the **Palace**, a surprisingly unassuming edifice built round an octagonal stair turret heightened last century to bear the castle's main flagpole. Begun in the 1430s, the palace's present Renaissance appearance is thanks to King James IV, though it was remodelled for Mary, Queen of Scots and her consort Henry, Lord Darnley, whose entwined initials (MAH), together with the date 1566, can be seen above one of the doorways. This gives access to a few historic rooms, the most interesting of which is the tiny panelled bedchamber at the extreme southeastern corner, where Mary gave birth to James VI. Along with the rest of the palace, the room was remodelled for James's triumphant homecoming in 1617. This was to be the last time it served as a royal residence.

THE PALACE |

13

Another section of the palace has been refurbished with a detailed audiovisual presentation on the **Honours of Scotland**, the originals of which are housed in the Crown Room at the very end of the display. These magnificent crown jewels – the only pre-Restoration set in the United Kingdom – serve as one of the most potent images of Scotland's nationhood. They were last used for the Scottish-only coronation of Charles II in 1651, an event which provoked the wrath of Oliver Cromwell, who attempted to have the jewels melted down. Having narrowly escaped his clutches by being smuggled out of the castle and hidden in a rural church, the jewels later served as symbols of the absent monarch at sittings of the Scottish Parliament before being locked away in a chest following the Union of 1707. For over a century they were out of sight and eventually presumed lost, before being rediscovered in 1818 as a result of a search initiated by Sir Walter Scott.

Of the three pieces comprising the Honours, the oldest is the **sceptre**, which bears statuettes of the Virgin and Child, St James and St Andrew, rounded off by a polished globe of rock crystal: it was given to James IV in 1494 by Pope Alexander VI, and refashioned by Scottish craftsmen for James V. Even finer is the **sword**, a swaggering Italian High Renaissance masterpiece by the silversmith Domenico da Sutri, presented to James IV by the great artistic patron Pope Julius II. Both the hilt and the scabbard are engraved with Julius's personal emblem, showing the oak tree and its acorns, the symbols of the risen Christ, together with dolphins, symbols of the Church. The jewel-encrusted **crown**, made for James V by the Scottish goldsmith James Mosman, incorporates the gold circlet worn by Robert the Bruce and is surmounted by an enamelled orb and cross.

The glass case containing the Honours has recently been rearranged to create space for its newest addition, the **Stone of Destiny**.

The Stone of Destiny

Legend has it that the Stone of Destiny (also called the Stone of Scone) was "Jacob's Pillow", on which Jacob dreamed of the ladder of angels connecting earth and heaven. Its real history is obscure, but it is known that it was moved from Ireland to Dunadd by missionaries, and thence to Dunstaffnage, from where Kenneth MacAlpine, king of the Dalriada Scots, brought it to the abbey at Scone in 838. There it remained for almost five hundred years and was used as a coronation throne on which all kings of Scotland were crowned.

In 1296, an over-eager Edward I stole what he believed to be the Stone and installed it at Westminster Abbey, where, apart from a brief interlude in 1950, when it was removed by Scottish nationalists and hidden in Arbroath, it remained for seven hundred years. All this changed in December 1996 when, after an elaborate ceremony-laden journey from London, the Stone returned to Scotland, one of many doomed attempts by the dying Conservative government to convince the Scottish people that the Union was a jolly good thing. Much to the annoyance of the people of Perth and the curators of Scone Palace, and to the general indifference of the Scottish public, the Stone was placed in Edinburgh Castle.

However, speculation surrounds the authenticity of the Stone, for the original is said to have been intricately carved, while the one seen today is a plain block of sandstone. Many believe that the canny monks at Scone palmed this off on to the English king and that the real Stone of Destiny lies hidden in an underground chamber, its whereabouts a mystery to all but a chosen few.

Around Crown Square

The south side of Crown Square is occupied by the **Great Hall**, built under James IV as a venue for banquets and other ceremonial occasions. Until 1639 the hall was the meeting place of the Scottish Parliament, it later underwent the indignity of conversion and subdivision, first into a barracks, then a hospital. During this time, its hammerbeam roof – the earliest of three in the Old Town – was hidden from view. It was restored towards the end of the last century, when the hall was decked out in the full-blown Romantic manner.

On the west side of the square, the eighteenth-century Queen Anne Barracks house part of the **Scottish United Services Museum**, with displays on each of the different Scottish military regiments, plus the navy and air force. Note the model of *The Great George*, a ship made by French prisoners incarcerated in the castle during the eighteenth and early nineteenth centuries.

In 1755, the castle church of St Mary on the north side of the square was replaced by a barracks, which in turn was skilfully converted into the quietly reverential **Scottish National War Memorial** in honour of the 150,000 Scots who fell in World War I.

The rest of the complex

From Crown Square, you can descend to the **Vaults**, a series of cavernous chambers erected by order of James IV to provide an even surface for the showpiece buildings above. They were later used as a prison for captured foreign nationals, who have bequeathed a rich legacy of graffiti, the most telling being the figure of "Lord Nord" (Lord North, prime minister during the American War of Independence), dangling from a gallows. One of the rooms houses the famous fifteenth-century siege gun, **Mons Meg**, which could fire a 500-pound stone nearly two miles. The gun was used in a number of sieges, but, because of its huge size, could only travel around three miles a day and was soon relegated to ceremonial status. A seventeenth-century visitor, the London poet John Taylor, commented: "It is so great within, that it was told me that a child was once gotten there." In 1754, Mons Meg was taken to the Tower of London, where it stayed till Sir Walter Scott persuaded George IV, on the occasion of his 1822 state visit to Scotland, to return it.

Directly opposite the entrance to the vaults is the **Military Prison**, built in 1842, when the design and function of jails was a major topic of public debate. Although generally used as a military prison, civilian offenders were also confined here during World War I, the most notable being the Marxist John Maclean, who was later to found the Workers' Republican Party. The cells, though designed for solitary confinement, are less forbidding than might be expected.

Finally, beyond the Governor's House, and overlooking the two-tier western defences, the late nineteenth-century **hospital** is a continuation of the Scottish United Services Museum.

THE ROYAL MILE

The **Royal Mile**, the name given to the ridge linking the castle with Holyrood, was described by Daniel Defoe in 1724, as "the largest, longest and finest street for Buildings and Number of Inhabitants, not in Bretain only, but in the World". Almost exactly a mile in length, it is divided into four separate streets – **Castlehill**, **Lawnmarket**, **Canongate** and **High Street**. From these, branching out in a herringbone pattern, a series of tightly packed closes and steep lanes are entered via archways known as pends.

After the construction of the New Town, the Royal Mile degenerated into a notorious slum, but has since shaken off that reputation, becoming once again a highly desirable place to live. Although marred by rather too many over-priced shops, it is still among the most evocative parts of the city, and one that particularly rewards detailed exploration.

CASTLEHILL

Map 3, C8.

The narrow uppermost stretch of the Royal Mile is known as **Castlehill**. Rising up behind the Art Nouveau Witches' Fountain (see p.11) is the picturesque **Ramsay Garden**, centring on the octagonal **Goose-Pie House**, home of the eighteenth-century poet Allan Ramsay. During the Jacobite rebellion of 1745, while Ramsay stayed safely away from the hurly-burly, it was used by Bonnie Prince Charlie's soldiers for shooting at the castle sentries. At the end of the nineteenth century, the building was acquired by **Patrick Geddes**, a proto-sociologist and town planner who wanted to bring the middle classes back to the main streets of the Old Town, to make "the dingy grey of our cities gain something of the pure azures and flash across its smoky wilderness the gleam of Renaissance hope". In order to attract the right sort of person, Geddes built a number of plush flats in Ramsay Garden. In later life, as his Scottish experiment floundered, he went off to pursue his ideals in Grenoble and India. His lasting legacy is the revival of the Old Town, and the student residences he established here are still in use today.

As you head down from the Esplanade, look up at the west gable end of **Cannonball House**, the first building on the southern side of Castlehill: according to folklore, the ball lodged high up on the wall was fired from a cannon during the Jacobite siege of the castle in 1745. A less romantic but more plausible explanation is that the ball marks the gravitation height of the city's first piped water supply, which came from the reservoir over the road. Alongside, the **Scotch Whisky Heritage Centre** (daily: June–Sept 9.30am–6pm; Oct–May 10am–5.30pm; £4.20) gives the lowdown on all aspects of Scotland's national beverage, featuring a gimmicky ride in a "barrel" through a series of uninspiring historical tableaux, plus a film on aspects of production and blending. It's worth popping into the shop, whose stock gives an idea of the sheer range and diversity of the drink, with dozens of different brands on sale.

CASTLEHILL

19

Across the road, at the top of Castlehill, the huge former reservoir for the Old Town has been converted into the **Edinburgh Old Town Weaving Centre** (daily 9am–5.30pm; £3). This commercial operation unashamedly goes for the tartan jugular as it guides you through the various stages of weaving, via some massive machinery and a few tableaux. Visitors can see the whole process of weaving before selecting their own tartan or even creating a new one. The Centre has a large shop and restaurant and also hosts Scottish evenings for a hefty £36 inclusive of food and Scottish musical accompaniment.

A few doors further along, the **Outlook Tower** (April–Oct Mon–Fri 9.30am–6pm, Sat & Sun 10am–6pm; Nov–March Mon–Fri 10am–5pm; £3.40) has been one of Edinburgh's top tourist attractions since 1853, when the original seventeenth-century tenement was equipped with a **camera obscura**. It makes a good introduction to the city: panoramic images are beamed on to a white table, accompanied by a running commentary. For the best views, visit at noon, when there are fewer shadows. The viewing balcony is one of Edinburgh's best vantage points, and there are exhibitions on pinhole photography, holography, Victorian photographs of the city, and topographic paintings made between 1780 and 1860.

A few steps further on is the **Assembly Hall**, meeting place of the annual General Assembly of the Church of Scotland and, during the Festival, an extraordinarily effective venue for large-scale drama, normally staging the most ambitious events on the programme. It was built in 1859 for the breakaway Free Church; the established church previously met at the **Tolbooth Kirk** across the road. Stunningly sited at the foot of Castlehill, the Victorian Gothic kirk is one of the most distinctive features of the Edinburgh skyline, thanks to its majestic spire, the highest in the city; vacated by its

Gaelic-speaking congregation in 1981, it is due be converted into a centre for the Festival, incorporating ticket sales, press facilities and a Festival Club. The church's superb neo-Gothic detailing is due to Augustus Pugin, co-architect of the Houses of Parliament in London.

LAWNMARKET

Map 3, D8.
Below the Tolbooth Kirk, the Royal Mile opens out into the much broader expanse of **Lawnmarket**, which, as its name suggests, was once the setting for a linen market – "lawn" is a corruption of "Laon", one of the major sources of the fabric. At its northern end is the entry to **Milne's Court**, whose excellently restored tenements now serve as student residences, and immediately beyond, **James Court**, one of Edinburgh's most fashionable addresses prior to the advent of the New Town, with David Hume and James Boswell among those who lived there.

Back on Lawnmarket itself, **Gladstone's Land** (April–Oct Mon–Sat 10am–5pm, Sun 2–5pm; £2.80) takes its name from the merchant Thomas Gledstane (sic), who in 1617 acquired a modest dwelling on the site, transforming it into a magnificent six-storey mansion. The Gledstane family are thought to have occupied the third floor, renting out the rest to merchants, in the style of tenement occupation still widespread in the city today. The arcaded ground floor, the only authentic example left of what was once a common feature of Royal Mile houses, has been restored to illustrate its early function as a shopping booth. Several other rooms have been kitted out in authentic period style to give an impression of the lifestyle of a well-to-do household of the late seventeenth century; the Painted Chamber, with its decorated wooden ceiling and wall friezes, is particularly impressive. Elsewhere, to underline the importance of trade with continental Europe and beyond, the building has Dutch and Chinese porcelain and seventeenth-century Dutch paintings by Jacob Ruisdael and others.

A few paces further on, steps lead down to Lady Stair's Close where you'll find **Lady Stair's House** (June–Sept Mon–Sat 10am–6pm; Oct–May Mon–Sat 10am–5pm; also Sun 2–5pm during Festival; free), named after the gorgeous and foul-mouthed eighteenth-century society figure on whose life Walter Scott based his story *My Aunt Margaret's Mirror*. Built in the 1620s, the house now contains a humdrum museum celebrating Scotland's literary trinity of Scott, Burns and Stevenson, a strange collection which hedges its bets with cases full of "said to be", "reputed to be" or even "similar to". There are assorted locks of hair, walking sticks and a few mementoes of Stevenson's stay in Samoa, plus some oddities such as an enamelled marble apple given by Robert Burns to his wife Jean Armour. Don't miss the painting, *Parliament Square and Public Characters of Edinburgh*, in the Burns Room, which gives a good idea of the layout of the area round St Giles in the eighteenth century.

Riddle's Close, on the south side of Lawnmarket, leads to **Riddle's Court**, where you'll find **MacMorran's Close** and the home of the Baillie MacMorran, a wealthy merchant who was killed in 1595 while attempting to quell a school riot: local boys barricaded themselves into the High School and demanded a week's holiday and when MacMorran came to sort them out he was shot through the head by William Sinclair, later to become Sir William Sinclair of Mey. Further down the street, **Brodie's Close** is named after the father of one of Edinburgh's most notorious characters, **Deacon William Brodie** (see box opposite) pillar of society by day, burglar by night.

Deacon Brodie

On the surface, **William Brodie**, wit, town councillor, cabinet-maker and head of the Incorporation of Wrights and Masons, was a honourable member of late eighteenth-century society. However, like many of his contemporaries he was involved in a variety of more lowly activities, bestowing his custom on cock-fights and various drinking clubs, where he indulged in a constant round of bingeing, gambling and womanizing. In order to fund these activities, he always carried a piece of putty which he would use to take an impression of any keys left hanging up in houses that he visited. Armed with a copy of the keys cut by a local blacksmith, Brodie then robbed the houses. After the audacious robbery of the Excise Office in Chessel's Court, which netted the dismal sum of £16, Brodie disappeared to Holland. One of his accomplices revealed his identity, Brodie was arrested and brought back to Edinburgh, where he was executed in 1788 on a gallows of his own making. Brodie remained blasé to the end, even writing an absurd will, which he ended with the dedication: "I recommend to all rogues, sharpers, thieves and gamblers, as well in high as in low stations, to take care of theirs by leaving of all wicked practices, and becoming good members of society."

Brodie has since provided the inspiration for many stories, notably Robert Louis Stevenson's *Dr Jekyll & Mr Hyde*. Rather more unexpectedly, Muriel Spark's Jean Brodie is described as a direct descendant of the disreputable Deacon.

PARLIAMENT SQUARE

Map 3, E9.

Lawnmarket ends at a crossroads of George IV Bridge and Bank Street, from here the Royal Mile becomes High Street, preceded by Parliament Square immediately on the right. The square is dominated by the High Kirk of St Giles

23

(see below) and by the continuous Neoclassical facades of the **Law Courts**. These were originally planned by Robert Adam (1728–92), one of four brothers in a family of architects (their father William Adam designed Hopetoun House; see p.77) whose work helped give the New Town much of its grace and elegance. Because of a shortage of funds, the present exteriors were built to designs by Robert Reid (1776–1856), the designer of the northern part of New Town, who faithfully quoted from Adam's architectural vocabulary without matching his flair. William Stark, a more flamboyant architect designed the **Signet Library**, which occupies the west side of the square. It has one of the most beautiful interiors in Edinburgh – its sumptuous colonnaded hall a perfect embodiment of the ideals of the Age of Reason. Unfortunately, it can only be seen by prior written application, except on very occasional open days.

Facing the southern side of St Giles, is **Parliament House**, built in the 1630s for the Scottish Parliament, a role it maintained until the Union, when it passed into the hands of the legal fraternity. Following the Union in 1707, the building became the centre of the Scottish legal profession – still its function today. Inside there are portraits, including several by Raeburn, and sculptures of the leading legal figures of the last few centuries, among them the figure of Duncan Forbes of Culloden, who helped to deal with the aftermath of the Jacobite rebellion of 1745, earning the disapproval of the notorious Duke of Cumberland who described him as "that old woman who talked to me about humanity". The most notable feature of the interior is the extravagant hammerbeam roof, and the delicately carved stone corbels from which it springs: in addition to some vicious grotesques, they include accurate depictions of several castles, including Edinburgh. Today Parliament House is readily accessible during the week, when it's used by lawyers and their clients for hushed conferrals in between court sittings.

Outside, on the square, is a life-size **equestrian statue of King Charles II** wearing the garb of a Roman emperor. Back on the High Street, beside a bloated memorial to the fifth Duke of Buccleuch, the brickwork pattern set in the pavement is known as the **Heart of Midlothian**. Immortalized in Scott's novel of the same name, it marks the site of a demolished Tolbooth; you may see passers-by spitting on it for luck. The **Mercat Cross**, at the eastern end of St Giles, was once the setting for public executions and more joyous events, such as the return from France of Mary, Queen of Scots in 1561, when the spouts of the cross were said to have flowed with wine. Little of what remains today is original: the cross collapsed in 1756, and was only rebuilt in 1885 with financial assistance from William Gladstone. (As with the Tolbooth, parts of the cross were installed at Abbotsford, the Borders home of Sir Walter Scott.) The site is still occasionally used for the reading out of Royal proclamations, such as the dissolution of Parliament.

High Kirk of St Giles

Map 3, E8. Easter–Sept Mon–Fri 9am–7pm, Sat & Sun 9am–5pm; Oct–Easter Mon–Sat 9am–5pm, Sun 1–5pm.

The **High Kirk of St Giles**, the sole parish church of medieval Edinburgh and where John Knox (see box on p.34) launched and directed the Scottish Reformation, is almost invariably referred to as a cathedral, although it has only been the seat of a bishop on two brief and unhappy occasions in the seventeenth century. According to one of the city's best-known legends, the attempt in 1637 to introduce the English prayer book, and thus episcopal government, so incensed a humble stallholder named Jenny Geddes that she hurled her

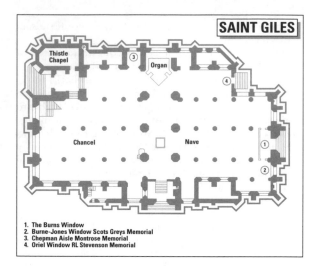

SAINT GILES

Thistle Chapel

③ Organ

④

Chancel

Nave

①

②

1. The Burns Window
2. Burne-Jones Window Scots Greys Memorial
3. Chepman Aisle Montrose Memorial
4. Oriel Window RL Stevenson Memorial

stool at the preacher, uttering the immortal words: "Out, out, does the false loon dare say Mass at my lugg [ear]?", thus prompting the rest of the congregation to chase the offending clergy out of the building. A tablet in the north aisle marks the spot from where she let rip.

In the early nineteenth century, St Giles received a much-needed but over-drastic restoration, covering most of the Gothic exterior with a smooth stone coating that gives it a certain Georgian dignity while sacrificing its medieval character almost completely. The only part to survive this treatment is the late fifteenth-century tower, whose resplendent crown spire is formed by eight flying buttresses.

The **interior** has survived in much better shape. Especially notable are the four massive piers supporting the tower, which date back, at least in part, to the church's

HIGH KIRK OF ST GILES

Norman predecessor. In the nineteenth century, St Giles was adorned with a whole series of funerary monuments in order to give it the character of a national pantheon on the model of Westminster Abbey. It was also equipped with several Pre-Raphaelite stained-glass windows. The best of these, designed by Edward Burne-Jones and William Morris, showing Old Testament prophets and the Israelites crossing the River Jordan, can be seen on the facade wall of the **north aisle**. Alongside is the great **west window**, which was dedicated to Robbie Burns in 1985 causing enormous controversy – as a hardened drinker and womanizer, the national bard was far from being an upholder of accepted Presbyterian values. Look out also for an elegant bronze relief of Robert Louis Stevenson (see box overleaf) on the south side of the church by the American, Augustus St Gaudens. The original design had the author reclining on a bed smoking a cigarette; he now lies on a chaise longue, pen in hand. Opposite is a memorial to the **Marquis of Montrose**, leader of the forces of Charles I in Scotland, who was executed and dismembered in 1650.

At the southeastern corner of St Giles, the **Thistle Chapel** was built by Sir Robert Lorimer in 1911 as the private chapel of the sixteen knights of the Most Noble Order of the Thistle. Self-consciously derivative of St George's Chapel in Windsor, it's an exquisite piece of craftsmanship, with an elaborate ribbed vault, huge drooping bosses and extravagantly ornate stalls.

HIGH STREET AND AROUND

Map 3, C0.

The third section of the Royal Mile proper is known as **High Street**, and occupies two blocks on either side of the intersection between North Bridge and South Bridge.

Robert Louis Stevenson

Born in Edinburgh into a distinguished family of engineers, **Robert Louis Stevenson** (1850–94) was a sickly child, with a solitary childhood dominated by his governess Alison "Cummie" Cunningham, who regaled him with tales drawn from Calvinist folklore. Sent to university to study engineering, Stevenson rebelled against his upbringing by spending much of his time with the city's lowlife and eventually switching to law. Although called to the bar in 1875, by then he had decided to channel his energies into literature.

While still a student, he had made his mark as an essayist, and he published in his lifetime over a hundred essays. Stevenson's other early successes were two **travelogues**, *An Inland Voyage* and *Travels with a Donkey in the Cevennes*, kaleidoscopic jottings based on his journeys in France, where he went to escape Scotland's bad weather. It was there that he met Fanny Osbourne, an American ten years his senior, who was estranged from her husband and had two children in tow. His voyage to join her in San Francisco formed the basis for his most important factual work, *The Amateur Emigrant*, a vivid first-hand account of the great nineteenth-century European migration to the United States.

Having married the now-divorced Fanny, Stevenson began an elusive search for an agreeable climate that led to Switzerland, the French Riviera and the Scottish Highlands. He belatedly turned to the **novel**, achieving immediate acclaim in 1881 for *Treasure Island*, a highly moralistic adventure yarn that began as an entertainment for his stepson and future collaborator, Lloyd Osbourne. In 1886, his most famous **short story**, *Dr Jekyll & Mr Hyde*, despite its nominal London setting, offered a vivid evocation of Edinburgh's Old Town; an allegory of its dual personality of prosperity and squalor, and an analysis of its Calvinistic preoccupations with guilt and damnation. The same year saw the publication of the historical romance, *Kidnapped*, an adventure novel which exemplified his view that literature should seek above all to entertain.

In 1887 Stevenson left Britain for good, travelling first to the United States where he began one of his most ambitious novels, *The Master of Ballantrae*. A year later, he set sail for the South Seas, and eventually settled in Samoa; his last works include a number of stories with a local setting, such as the grimly realistic *The Ebb Tide* and *The Beach of Falesà*. However, Scotland continued to be his main inspiration: he wrote *Catriona* as a sequel to *Kidnapped*, and was at work on two more novels with Scottish settings, *St Ives* and *Weir of Hermiston*, a dark story of father son confrontation, at the time of his sudden death from a brain homorrhage in 1894. He was buried on the top of Mount Vaea overlooking the Pacific Ocean.

Directly opposite the Mercat Cross, the U-shaped **City Chambers** were designed by John Adam, brother of Robert, as the Royal Exchange. Local traders never warmed to the exchange, however, so the town council established its headquarters there instead. Amazingly, the rear of the building has twelve storeys to accommodate the sharp drop onto Cockburn Street.

Beneath the city chambers lies **Mary King's Close** (tours daily: 10.30 & 11.30am, 2.30, 3.30, 4 30, 8.30 & 9.30pm; closed Sun morning & Tues evening; £5), one of Edinburgh's most unusual attractions. Built in the early sixteenth century, it was closed off for many years after the devastation of the 1645 plague, before being entirely covered up by the chambers in 1753. During World War II, parts of the close were brought back into public use as an air-raid shelter, but today it's a popular tourist attraction. For many years tours of the close were occasional and sporadic, but are now taking place more frequently (contact *Mercat Tours* on ☏661 4541 for details). A little further down the street is **Anchor Close**, site of the printing works of William Smellie, who published the first ever edition of the *Encyclopedia Britannica* there in 1768.

At the junction of the south side of High Street and South Bridge stands the **Tron Kirk**, for many years the focal point for Hogmanay revellers, until today's organized events shifted the crowds to other parts of the city. Built in the 1630s to house the congregation evicted from St Giles when the latter became the seat of a bishop, the church doesn't have a happy history: the south aisle was removed in the late eighteenth century in order to make room for the South Bridge, and the original spire was destroyed in the Great Fire of 1824, leading Sir Walter Scott to remark, "Mony a wearie, wearie sermon hae I heard beneath that steeple!" The Tron remained in use as a church until 1952 and was then closed for forty years before reopening as the **Old Town Information Centre.**

....

**For details of the Old Town Information Centre
phone ☏557 1700.**

....

Excavations within the church have revealed sections of an old close, **Marlin's Wynd**. The cobbled steps and the traces of old foundations on the wynd, which formerly contained bookshops and markets, are highly evocative of Edinburgh's past, making this an essential stop on the Royal Mile. In the same building, the **Edinburgh Old Town Renewal Trust** presents a series of informative displays on the history of the Old Town.

Beyond the intersection of North Bridge and South Bridge back on the northern side of High Street, is **Paisley Close**, above whose entrance is a bust of a youth with the inscription "Heave awa' chaps, I'm no' dead yet", uttered in 1861 by a boy trapped by rubble following the collapse of a tenement in the close, and who was subsequently dug out by rescue workers.

In **Chalmer's Close**, just to the east, **Trinity Apse** is a poignant reminder of the fifteenth-century Holy Trinity Collegiate Church, formerly one of Edinburgh's most outstanding buildings, but demolished in 1848 to make way for an extension to Waverley Station. The stones were carefully numbered and stored on Calton Hill so that it could be reassembled at a later date, but many were pilfered before sufficient funds became available, and only the apse could be reconstructed on this new site. The problem in recent years has been to find a suitable use for what is still an impressive building. It's now a **Brass Rubbing Centre** (June–Sept Mon–Sat 10am–6pm; Oct–May Mon–Sat 10am–5pm; only Sun 2–5pm during the Festival; free), where you can rub your own impressions from Pictish crosses for around 40p.

On the other side of the High Street, the **Museum of Childhood** (same opening hours as Brass Rubbing Centre; free), was founded by an eccentric local councillor who disliked children. Although he claimed that the museum was a serious social archive for adults, it has always attracted swarms of kids, who delight in the dolls' house, teddy bears, marionettes and other paraphernalia. The founder's quirky sense of humour comes over on some of the captions for exhibits and even more so in his unendearing wish to have a memorial window in honour of **King Herod** placed at the museum's entrance.

Opposite the museum is **Moubray House** (closed to the public), probably the city's oldest surviving dwelling, built around 1462. It provided lodging for **Daniel Defoe** who stayed in the capital as a propaganda agent for the English in 1706 prior to the Act of Union.

Just past John Knox's House, on what is termed the "knuckle" of the High Street, is the Netherbow Centre, a theatre with an excellent café (see p.158).

John Knox's House

Map 3, G8. Mon–Sat 10am–4.30pm; £1.75.

Next door to Moubray House is the much-photographed **John Knox's House**, a three-storeyed building with distinctive wooden balconies projecting out into the High Street. With its outside stairway, Biblical motto and sundial adorned with a statue of Moses, it gives a good impression of how the Royal Mile must have once looked. Thought to have been built around the beginning of the sixteenth century, it was partially destroyed by English soldiers in 1544, and has since been restored many times. Although Knox is thought to have stayed here between 1560 and 1572, the link may stem solely from a period at the end of the eighteenth century, when the house was known as "Knox the Booksellers". James Mosman, royal goldsmith to Mary, Queen of Scots, certainly did reside in the house: the initials IM and MA (Mosman and his wife Mariota Arres) are still visible on the outer west wall of the building. The rather bare **interior**, which give a good idea of the labyrinthine layout of Old Town houses, contains a sparse **museum** displaying explanatory material on Knox's life and career, including early editions of works by him (such as the inimitably titled *Answer to a Great Number of Blasphemous Cavillations*) and other notable contemporaries. In recognition of the building's connection with James Mosman, there's a mock-up of a goldsmith's workroom on the first floor. On the second floor, there are fireplaces with attractive, albeit somewhat haphazardly positioned, Dutch tiles, wood-panelled walls and painted ceilings which together create a passable replica of a sixteenth-century town house.

CANONGATE

Map 3, H8.

For over 700 years, the district through which **Canongate** runs was a burgh in its own right, officially separate from the capital. Since the 1950s, much effort has been expended in restoring the area's many run-down buildings. On the northern side of the street, as you walk towards Holyrood, look out for two large tenements, **Shoemaker's Land** at no. 197 and **Bible Land** at nos. 183-7, both erected in the heyday of the Old Town by the Incorporation of Cordiners, one of Edinburgh's powerful guilds: the Cordiners' emblem of a crowned shoemaker's knife flanked by cherubs' heads appears above both buildings. Restoration work is still going on in the Canongate area, the latest project being the redevelopment of a massive area of derelict land, formerly occupied by breweries, and other industries round the eastern end of the south side.

Near the top of the Canongate on the southern side is **Chessel's Court** a mid-eighteenth century development with fanciful Rococo chimneys. It is best known as the location of the long-vanished Excise Office – the scene of the robbery that led to the eventual arrest and execution of Deacon Brodie (see box on p.23).

Dominated by a turreted steeple, the late sixteenth-century **Canongate Tolbooth** (June–Sept Mon Sat 10am–6pm; Oct–May 10am–5pm; also Sun 2–5pm during Festival; free), a little further down the north side of the street, has served both as the headquarters of the burgh administration

CANONGATE

John Knox

The Protestant reformer **John Knox** was born sometime between 1505 and 1514 in East Lothian, and trained for the priesthood at St Andrews University. Ordained in 1540, Knox then served as a private tutor, in league with Scotland's first significant Protestant leader, **George Wishart**. After Wishart was burned at the stake for heresy in 1546, Knox became involved with the group who had carried out the revenge murder of the Scottish Primate, Cardinal David Beaton, subsequently taking over his castle in St Andrews. The following year, this was captured by the French, and Knox was carted off to work as a galley slave.

He was freed in 1548, as a result of the intervention of the English, who invited him to play an evangelizing role in the spread of their own Reformation. When the Catholic Mary Tudor acceded to the English throne in 1553, Knox fled to the Continent, ending up as minister to the English-speaking community in Geneva, which was then in the grip of the theocratic government of **Jean Calvin**. Knox was quickly won over to his radical version of Protestantism, declaring Geneva to be "the most perfect school of Christ since the days of the Apostles". It was in Geneva that he wrote his most infamous treatise, *The First Blast of the Trumpet Against the Monstrous Regiment of Women*, an attack on the three Catholic women then ruling Scotland, England and France.

When Knox was allowed to return to Scotland in 1555, he took over as spiritual leader of the Reformation, becoming minister of St Giles in Edinburgh. He rigorously championed an alliance with Elizabeth I, which in the event proved crucial to the establishment of Protestantism as the official religion of Scotland in 1560: the deployment of English troops against the French garrison in Edinburgh dealt a fatal blow to Franco-

Spanish hopes of re-establishing Catholicism in both Scotland and England. Although the return of Mary, Queen of Scots the following year placed a Catholic monarch on the Scottish throne, reputedly Knox was always able to retain the upper hand in his famous disputes with her.

Before his death in 1572, Knox began mapping out the organization of the Scots Kirk, sweeping away all vestiges of episcopal control and giving laymen a role of unprecedented importance. He also proposed a nationwide education system, to be compulsory for the very young, and free for the poor; though lack of funds meant this could not be implemented in full. His final legacy was the posthumously published *History of the Reformation of Religion In the Realm of Scotland*, a justification of his life's work.

and as a prison, and now houses **The People's Story**, a lively museum devoted to the everyday life and work of Edinburgh people down the centuries, with sounds and tableaux on various aspects of city living – including a typical Edinburgh pub. Next door, **Canongate Kirk** was built in the 1680s to house the congregation expelled from Holyrood Abbey (see p.41) when the latter was commandeered by James VII (James II in England) to serve as the chapel for the Order of the Thistle. It's a curiously archaic design, still Renaissance in outline, and built to a cruciform plan wholly at odds with the ideals and requirements of Protestant worship. Its churchyard, one of the city's most exclusive cemeteries, commands a superb view across to Calton Hill. Among those buried here are Adam Smith, Mrs Agnes McLehose (better known as Robert Burns's "Clarinda") and Robert Fergusson, regarded by some as Edinburgh's greatest poet, despite his death at the age of 24; his headstone was donated by Burns, a fervent admirer, who also wrote the inscription.

CANONGATE

Directly opposite the Canongate Church lies **Huntly House** (June–Sept Mon–Sat 10am–6pm; Oct–May Mon–Sat 10am–5pm; also Sun 2–5pm during Festival; free). The main building which dates back to the late sixteenth century, was bought by the Incorporation of Hammermen in 1647 and converted into flats. It was restored in 1927 and since then it has served as a museum of local history. Exhibits include a quirky array of old shop signs, some dating back to the eighteenth century, as well as displays on indigenous industries such as glass, silver, pottery and clock-making, and on the career of Earl Haig. Also on view is the original version of the National Covenant of 1638; modern science has failed to resolve whether or not some of the signatories signed with their own blood, as tradition has it.

Among the several fine seventeenth-century mansions on the easternmost stretch of Canongate, **Panmure House** was for a time the home of Adam Smith, father of the science of political economy and unwitting guru of latter-day Conservatism. At the very foot of the street, the entrance to the residential **Whitehorse Close** was once the site of the inn from where stagecoaches began the journey to London. Stridently quaint, it drips with all the most characteristic features of Scottish vernacular architecture, crow-stepped gables, dormer windows, overhanging upper storeys and curving outside stairways.

CANONGATE

HOLYROODHOUSE TO CRAIGMILLAR

A t the foot of Canongate lies **Holyrood**, Edinburgh's royal quarter, the legend of whose foundation in 1128 is described in a fifteenth-century manuscript which is still kept there. The story goes that King David I, son of Malcolm III and St Margaret, went out hunting one day and was suddenly confronted by a stag who threw him from his horse and seemed ready to gore him. In desperation, the king tried to protect himself by grasping its antlers, but instead found himself holding a crucifix, whereupon the animal ran off. In a dream that night, he heard a voice commanding him to "make a house for Canons devoted to the Cross"; he duly obeyed, naming the abbey Holyrood ("rood" being an alternative name for a cross). More likely, however, is that David, the most pious of all Scotland's monarchs, simply acquired a relic of the True Cross and decided to build a suitable home for it.

Holyrood soon became a favoured **royal residence**, its situation in a secluded valley making it far more agreeable than the draughty castle. Originally it served as a guest house for **Holyrood Abbey**, a twelfth-century Augustinian foundation to which a wing for the exclusive use of the court was added during the reign of James II. This was transformed into a full-blown palace for James IV, which in turn was replaced by a much larger building for Charles II, although he never actually lived there. Indeed, it was something of a white elephant until Queen Victoria started making regular trips to her northern kingdom, a custom that has been maintained by her successors.

Beyond the palace grounds lies the marvellous **Holyrood Park**, a large area of semi-wild parkland in which several not too taxing walks along gentle slopes lead to peaceful lochs and the summit of **Arthur's Seat**, an extinct volcano, from where stupendous views abound. One destination is the attractive village of **Duddingston**, home to a twelfth-century parish church and the house in which Bonnie Prince Charlie is reputed to have spent the night before the battle of Prestonpans.

Two miles south of here is the picturesque **Craigmillar Castle**, in which the murder of Lord Darnley, husband of Mary, Queen of Scots, is said to have been planned.

THE PRECINCTS

On the north side of **Abbey Strand**, which forms a sort of processional way linking Canongate with Holyrood, **Abbey Lairds** is a four-storey sixteenth-century mansion which once served as a home for aristocratic debtors and is now occupied by royal flunkies during the summer seat of the court.

Legend has it that Mary, Queen of Scots used to bathe in sweet white wine in the curious little turreted structure nearby known as **Queen Mary's Bath House**; it is more likely, however, that it was either a summer pavilion or a dovecote. Its architecture is mirrored in the **Croft an**

Righ, a picturesque L-shaped house in a quiet, generally overlooked corner beside the eastern wall of the complex. The eastern edge of the palace grounds was formerly a debtor's sanctuary, known as St Anne's Yards, housing over a hundred residents in the early nineteenth century.

THE PALACE OF HOLYROODHOUSE

Map 6, B3. Daily: April–Oct 9.30am–5.15pm; Nov–March 9.30am–3.45pm; £5.20.

In its present form, the **Palace of Holyroodhouse** is largely a seventeenth-century creation, planned for Charles II. However, the tower house of the old palace was skilfully incorporated to form the northwestern block, with a virtual mirror image of it erected as a counterbalance at the other end. The three-storey **courtyard** is an early exercise in Palladian style, exhibiting a punctilious knowledge of the rules of classics to create a sense of absolute harmony and unity.

Inside, the **State Apartments**, as Charles II's palace is known, are decked out with oak panelling, tapestries, portraits and decorative paintings, all overshadowed by the magnificent white stucco **ceilings**, especially in the Morning Drawing Room where portraits of Bonnie Prince Charlie and George IV, loser and winner, hang side by side. The most eye-catching chamber, however, is the **Great Gallery**, which takes up the entire first floor of the northern wing. During the 1745 sojourn of the Young Pretender this was the setting for a banquet, described in detail in Scott's novel *Waverley*, and it is still used for big ceremonial occasions.

Holyrood is a working palace and the buildings are closed to the public at certain times for state functions, usually for a fortnight in the middle of May, and the first two weeks in July. At quiet times of the year, **free guided tours** are conducted by the palace's staff.

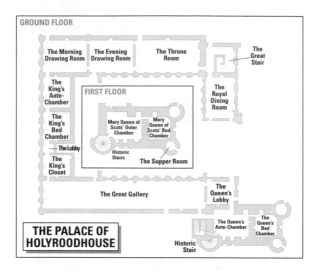

GROUND FLOOR

The Morning Drawing Room • The Evening Drawing Room • The Throne Room • The Great Stair

The King's Ante-Chamber

FIRST FLOOR

The Royal Dining Room

The King's Bed Chamber

Mary Queen of Scots' Outer Chamber • Mary Queen of Scots' Bed Chamber

The Lobby

Historic Stairs • The Supper Room

The King's Closet

The Great Gallery

The Queen's Lobby

THE PALACE OF HOLYROODHOUSE

The Queen's Ante-Chamber • The Queen's Bed Chamber

Historic Stair

Along the walls are 89 portraits commissioned from the seventeenth-century Dutch artist Jacob de Wet to illustrate the royal lineage of Scotland from its mythical origins in the fourth century BC; the result is unintentionally hilarious, as it is clear that the artist's imagination was taxed to bursting point by the need to paint so many different facial types without having an inkling as to what the subjects actually looked like. Legend has it that the artist trawled the streets of the Old Town for sitters to provide faces for the early obscure figures. In the adjacent **King's Closet**, de Wet's *The Finding of Moses* provides a biblical link to the portraits, the Scottish royal family claiming descent from Scota, the Egyptian pharaoh's daughter who discovered Moses in the bulrushes.

The oldest parts of the palace, the **Historical Apartments**, are mainly of note for their associations with

Mary, Queen of Scots and in particular for the brutal murder, organized by her husband, Lord Darnley, of her private secretary, David Rizzio, who was stabbed 56 times and dragged from the small closet, through the **Queen's Bedchamber**, and into the **Outer Chamber**. Until a few years ago, visitors were shown apparently indelible bloodstains on the floor of the latter, but these are now admitted to be fakes and have been covered up. A display cabinet in the same room shows some pieces of **needlework** woven by the deposed queen while in English captivity; another case has an outstanding **miniature portrait** of her by the French court painter, François Clouet.

HOLYROOD ABBEY

Map 6, C2.

In the grounds of the palace are the wonderfully evocative ruins of **Holyrood Abbey**. Of King David's original Norman church, the only surviving fragment is a doorway in the far southeastern corner. Most of the remainder dates from a late twelfth- and early thirteenth-century rebuilding in the Early Gothic style.

The surviving parts of the **west front**, including one of the twin towers and the elaborately carved entrance portal, show how resplendent the abbey must once have been. Unfortunately, its sacking by the English in 1547, followed by the demolition of the transept and chancel during the Reformation, all but destroyed the building. Charles I attempted to restore some semblance of unity by ordering the erection of the great east window and a new stone roof, but the latter collapsed in 1768, causing grievous damage to the rest of the structure. By this time, the Canongate congregation had another place of worship, and schemes to rebuild the abbey were abandoned.

HOLYROOD ABBEY

HOLYROOD PARK

Map 6.

Holyrood Park, or **Queen's Park** – a natural wilderness in the very heart of the modern city – is unquestionably one of Edinburgh's main assets, as locals (though relatively few tourists) readily appreciate. Packed into an area no more than five miles in diameter is an amazing variety of landscapes – mountains, crags, moorland, marshes, glens, lochs and fields – representing something of a microcosm of Scotland's scenery. The **Queen's Drive** circumnavigates the park, enabling many of its features to be seen by car, though you really need to stroll around to appreciate it fully.

Opposite the southern gates of the palace a pathway, nicknamed the Radical Road, traverses the ridge immediately below the **Salisbury Crags**, one of the main features of the Edinburgh skyline. Even though there is no path, you can walk along the top of the basalt crags, from where there are excellent views of the Palace of Holyroodhouse and Holyrood Abbey.

Following Queen's Drive in the other direction, you arrive at **St Margaret's Loch**, a nineteenth-century man-made pond, above which stand the scanty ruins of **St Anthony's Chapel**, another fine vantage point. From here, the road's loop is one-way only, ascending to **Dunsapie Loch**, again an artificial stretch of water, which makes an excellent foil to the eponymous crag behind. .

Arthur's Seat

Map 6, D6.

Arthur's Seat, a majestic extinct volcano rising 823ft above sea level, is Edinburgh's single most prominent landmark, resembling a huge crouched lion when seen from the west. As there is little reason to associate it with the British king of the Holy Grail legends, there's no satisfactory story to explain the name, though it may derive from the Gaelic phrase *Ard-na-Said*, meaning "Height of Arrows", from the days when the area was used as a hunting ground.

The climb from Dunsapie, up a grassy slope, followed by a rocky path near the summit, is considerably less arduous than it looks, and is a fairly straightforward twenty-minute walk, though there are several other, somewhat longer and more taxing ways up from other points in the park. The views from the top are all you'd expect, covering the entire city and much of the Firth of Forth; on a clear day, you can even see the southernmost mountains of the Highlands. The composer Felix Mendelssohn climbed Arthur's Seat in July 1829, noting: "It is beautiful here! In the evening a cool breeze is wafted from the sea, and then all objects appear clearly and sharply defined against the gray sky; the lights from the windows glitter brilliantly"

DUDDINGSTON

Map 6, I6.

From the foot of Salisbury Crags, there's a road which makes a sharp switchback, passing beneath **Samson's Ribs**, a group of basalt pillars strikingly reminiscent of the Hebridean island of Staffa. It continues on to **Duddingston Loch**, the only natural stretch of water in the park, now a bird sanctuary. Perched above it, just outside the park boundary, **Duddingston Kirk** dates back in part to the twelfth century and serves as the focus of one of the most unspoiled old villages within modern Edinburgh. In the gateway is a *loupin-on-stane*, a platform for mounting a horse, and *jougs*, an iron collar and chain set into the wall for humiliating offenders. According to tradition, Bonnie Prince Charlie stayed in **no. 8 Duddingston Causeway**, a plain-looking house built in 1721, on the night before his success at the battle of Prestonpans in 1745. Duddingston can be reached on foot through Holyrood Park; after a drink in the Sheep Heid (see p.148) take bus #42/46 from Duddingston Road West in either direction to get back to the city centre.

CRAIGMILLAR CASTLE

Map 6, G7. April–Sept Mon–Sat 9.30am–6pm, Sun 2–6pm; Oct–March Mon–Wed & Sat 9.30am–4pm, Thurs 9.30am–noon, Sun 2–4pm; £1.50.

Roughly two miles southeast of Duddingston lies **Craigmillar Castle**, one of Queen Mary's favourite residences and still a formidable sight marred only by the proximity of the ugly council housing scheme of Craigmillar, one of Edinburgh's most deprived districts.

The oldest part of the complex is the L-shaped **tower house**, which dates back to the early 1600s: it remains substantially intact, and the great hall, with its resplendent late Gothic chimneypiece, is in good enough shape to be rented out for functions. Of particular interest is the kitchen with a drain and service hatch and a dungeon in which a skeleton was discovered in 1813.

A few decades after Craigmillar's completion, the tower house was surrounded by a quadrangular wall with cylindrical corner towers pierced by some of the earliest surviving gunholes in Britain. The west range was remodelled as an aristocratic mansion in the mid-seventeenth century, but its owners abandoned the place a hundred years later, leaving it to decay into picturesque ruin.

Take bus #14, #42 or #46 from the city centre to the junction of Duddingston Road West and Peffermill Road, from where the castle is a ten-minute walk along Craigmillar Castle Road.

COWGATE TO THE UNIVERSITY

Cowgate, the main thoroughfare of the Old Town south of the Royal Mile, is today a somewhat gloomy street during the daytime containing little of interest with the exceptions of **St Cecilia's Hall** and the **Magdalen Chapel**. In the last decade or so Cowgate has experienced something of a revival, though few tourists venture here except in the evening, when the area really comes to life thanks to its numerous pubs and clubs. The western end of the street leads to the wide open space of **Grassmarket**, the scene of many grisly events in the city's history, while to the south stand **Greyfriars Kirk** and the **Royal Museum of Scotland**, which covers an amazing miscellany of themes and a timescale which spans from fossils to modern technology. A short distance from here is the **University of Edinburgh**, home to the **Talbot Rice Gallery,** a venue for good exhibitions and a permanent showcase for some fine Dutch paintings.

COWGATE

Map 3, H3.

One of Edinburgh's oldest surviving streets, **Cowgate** was formerly one of the city's most prestigious addresses. However, with the construction of the South and George IV bridges to provide a link between the Old and New towns, Cowgate was entombed below street level; the water supply for the Old Town was diverted to serve the new residences, resulting in severe shortage in the lower parts of the old city which caused sporadic outbreaks of cholera in the 1840s. Hans Christian Andersen, who visited the city around this time, wrote, "poverty and misery seem to peep out of the open hatches which normally serve as windows". The area was once known as the "Irish Quarter" after the thousands of immigrants who swarmed into the area to escape the Great Famine of 1846.

St Cecilia's Hall

Map 3, G3. Wed & Sat 2–5pm; Mon–Sat 10.30am–12.30pm during Festival; £3.

Standing at the corner of the Cowgate and Niddry Street, **St Cecilia's Hall** is Scotland's oldest purpose-built concert hall. Established for the Musical Society of Edinburgh in 1763, the hall thrived until the emergence of the New Town attracted concert-goers away from the area. After a spell as a Masonic Lodge, it was purchased by Edinburgh University in 1966.

For St Cecilia's Hall box office details, see p.152.

Externally the building looks unexciting: the original entrance on Niddry Street is blackened with Old Town grime and the new one created by the restoration of the 1960s resembles a public toilet. Inside, however, it's a beautiful shallow-domed structure, which has been restored and extended to house the **Russell Collection** of antique keyboard instruments, comprising a variety of virginals, spinets, clavichords and harpsichords, most of which are in working order – as staff will happily demonstrate. At present the collection is very low-key, but there are plans to upgrade it with the help of funding from the Lottery over the next few years.

Magdalen Chapel

Map 3, E4. Mon–Fri 9.30am–4.30pm; free.

Towards the western end of Cowgate stands the **Magdalen Chapel**, which was built between 1541 and 1544 with money bequeathed by Michael MacQueen, a prominent citizen, and topped up by his widow, Janet Rynd, whose tomb is discreetly positioned in the southeast corner. After her death, patronage of the almshouse chapel passed to the Incorporation of Hammermen, a guild to which most Edinburgh metal workers, other than goldsmiths, belonged. One of the focal points of the Reformation, it was probably the setting for the first ever General Assembly of the Church of Scotland.

The Hammermen added a handsome tower and steeple in the 1620s, and later transformed the chapel into their guildhall, which was suitably adorned with fine ironwork. The most important feature of the chapel is a set of four brilliantly coloured heraldic roundels on the south wall, the only pre-Reformation stained glass in Scotland to have survived in situ. Look out for the lower-left-hand roundel, depicting the arms of the MacQueen family, which bizarrely contains the heads of several savages.

The chapel has seen a variety of uses over the centuries: from serving as a mortuary for the bodies of Covenanters (see box on p.50) hanged in the Grassmarket, to being used to display mechanical curiosities in the eighteenth century and, latterly, as the base of the Edinburgh Medical Missionary Society. Recent restoration of the chapel, now used occasionally for concerts, has reversed a long-term decline.

GRASSMARKET

Map 3, C4.

At its western end, Cowgate opens out into **Grassmarket**, which has played an important role in the murkier aspects of Edinburgh's turbulent history. The public gallows were located here, and it was the scene of numerous riots and other disturbances down the centuries. It was here, for example, in 1736, that Captain Porteous was lynched after he had ordered shots to be fired at the crowd watching a public execution. The notorious body snatchers William Burke and William Hare had their lair in a now-vanished close just off the western end of Grassmarket, luring to it victims whom they murdered with the intention of selling their bodies to the eminent physician Robert Knox. Eventually, Hare betrayed his partner, who was duly executed in 1829, and Knox's career was finished off as a result. Today, Grassmarket can still be seamy, though the cluster of busy bars and restaurants along its northern side are evidence of a serious attempt to clean up its image.

At the northeastern corner of Grassmarket are five old tenements of the old **West Bow**, which formerly zigzagged up to the Royal Mile. The rest of this was replaced in the 1840s by the curving **Victoria Street**, an unusual two-tier thoroughfare, with arcaded shops below, and a pedestrian terrace above. This sweeps up to **George IV Bridge** and the **National Library of Scotland** (Mon–Sat 10am–5pm, Sun 2–5pm; free) which holds a rich collection of illuminated manuscripts, early printed books, historical documents, and the letters and papers of prominent Scottish literary figures, displayed in regularly changing thematic exhibitions.

THE GREYFRIARS AREA

Map 3, E5.

At the southwestern corner of George IV Bridge stands the **statue of Greyfriars Bobby**, which must rank as Edinburgh's most sentimental tourist attraction. Bobby was a Skye terrier acquired as a working dog by a police constable named John Gray. When the latter died in 1858, Bobby began a vigil on his grave which he maintained until he died fourteen years later. In the process, he became an Edinburgh celebrity, fed and cared for by locals who gave him a special collar (now in the Huntly House Museum; see p.36) to prevent him being impounded as a stray. His statue, originally a fountain, was modelled from life, and erected soon after his death; his story has gained international renown, thanks to a spate of cloying books and tear-jerking movies.

The grave Bobby mourned over is in the **Greyfriars Kirkyard**, which among its clutter of grandiose seventeenth- and eighteenth century funerary monuments is the striking mausoleum of the Adam family of architects in which many famous figures are buried, including the poet and bestseller **Allan Ramsay Senior** and **James Craig**, designer of the New Town. Greyfriars is most closely associated, however, with the long struggle to establish Presbyterianism in Scotland: in 1638, it was the setting for the signing of the National Covenant, while in 1679 some 1200 Covenanters were imprisoned in the enclosure at the southwestern end of the yard. Set against the northern wall is the **Martyrs' Monument**, a defiantly worded memorial commemorating all those who died in pursuit of the eventual victory.

THE GREYFRIARS AREA

The Covenanters

When Charles I, inspired by his belief in the divine right of kings, sought to impose a new *Book of Common Prayer* on the Scottish people in 1637, reaction was predictably strong. Fuelled by anger at such high-handed interference, the **National Covenant**, calling for "a glorious marriage of the kingdom and God", was signed in Greyfriars Kirkyard the following year by around 5000 people, and subsequently by some 300,000 across Scotland. In November 1638 the General Assembly of the Church of Scotland, meeting for the first time in twenty years, proscribed Charles's Prayer Book and denounced his Episcopalian reforms. **The Covenanters**, under the leadership of the Earl of Argyll, now administered Scotland. With the outbreak of the Civil War in England they forged links with the English opposition to Charles though the **Solemn League and Covenant** of 1643.

Following the execution of Charles I in 1649, Charles II made amends for his father's errors by signing the Covenant before his coronation as King of Scotland at Scone in January 1651. By then, however, Charles was a side issue, Oliver Cromwell having defeated the Scottish army at the battle of Dunbar and having captured Edinburgh Castle.

After the Restoration of the monarchy in 1660, it was the turn of Charles II to interfere in Scottish religious affairs. He reneged on his signing of the Covenant and sought to reintroduce episcopacy. The Covenanters fled, holding prayer meetings outdoors in **conventicles**: They were subject to fierce repression for many years, with an estimated 1800 losing their lives. After the battle of **Bothwell Bridge** in the west of Scotland in 1679, around 1200 Covenanters were detained in Greyfriars Kirkyard for four months. Given only the most rudimentary shelter, many died. Some who promised not to rebel again were released and the remainder were put on a ship for Barbados, which sank off the Orkney Islands leaving only forty survivors. Covenanter resistance weakened after this point with only a hard core, known as the Cameronians, surviving into the eighteenth century.

In the northeast corner of the Greyfriars Kirkyard there is a monument to the Covenanters, erected in 1706, with an inscription added in 1771, part of which reads:

"Here lies interr'd the dust of those who stood,
'Gainst perjury, resisting unto blood".

An example of a *mort safe*, a lockable iron structure designed to deter grave-robbers, can be seen beside the path running along the south side of the church. After the founding of Edinburgh University, a shortage of bodies to use for dissection led to grave-robbing, and as early as 1711, more than 100 years before the heyday of Burke and Hare, the Royal College of Surgeons reported: "of late there has been a violation of sepulchres in the Greyfriars Churchyard by some who most unchristianly have been stealing, or at least attempting to carry away, the bodies of the dead out of their graves".

The graveyard rather overshadows **Greyfriars Kirk** itself, completed in 1620 as the first new church in Edinburgh since the Reformation. It's a real oddball in both layout and design, having a nave and aisles but no chancel, and adopting the anachronistic architectural language of the friary that preceded it, complete with medieval-looking windows, arches and buttresses.

At the western end of Greyfriars Kirkyard is one of the most significant surviving portions of the **Flodden Wall**, the city fortifications erected in the wake of Scotland's disastrous military defeat of 1513. When open, the gateway beyond offers a short cut to **George Heriot's Hospital**, otherwise approached from Lauriston Place to the south. Founded as a

THE GREYFRIARS AREA

home for poor boys by "Jinglin Geordie" Heriot, James VI's goldsmith, it is now one of Edinburgh's most prestigious fee-paying schools; although you can't go inside, you can wander round the quadrangle, whose array of towers, turrets, chimneys, carved doorways and traceried windows is one of the finest achievements of the Scottish Renaissance.

THE ROYAL MUSEUM OF SCOTLAND

Map 3, F5. Mon–Sat 10am–5pm, Sun noon–5pm; free.

On the south side of Chambers Street, which runs east from Greyfriars Bobby, stands the **Royal Museum of Scotland**, a dignified Venetian-style palace with a cast-iron interior modelled on that of the Crystal Palace in London. Intended as Scotland's answer to the museum complex in London's South Kensington, it contains an extraordinarily eclectic range of exhibits; the scope will be broader still after the completion of a huge annexe in 1998, when many items previously kept either in storage or at the **Museum of Antiquities** will be displayed. Among the most precious items to look out for in the new annexe are artefacts from the **prehistoric, Roman** and **Viking** eras and the famous **ivory chessmen** from the island of Lewis.

The museum has a noisy café at the rear, and a rather calmer one in the entrance hall.

The **sculpture** in the lofty entrance hall begins with a superb Assyrian relief from the royal palace at Nimrud, and ranges via Classical Greece, Rome and Nubia to buddhas from Japan and Burma and a totem pole from British Columbia. Also on the ground floor are collections of stuffed animals and birds, and a predominantly hands-on **technology** section featuring classic pieces of machinery of the Industrial Revolution. These include a double-action beam engine designed by James Watt in 1786; the *Wylam Dilly* of 1813, twin of the *Puffing Billy*; and the 1896 *Hawk Glider*, the earliest British flying machine.

Upstairs there's a fine array of Egyptian mummies, ceramics from ancient Greece to the present day, costumes, jewellery, natural-history displays and a splendid selection of European decorative art ranging from early medieval liturgical objects via Limoges enamels and sixteenth-century German woodcarving to stunning **French silverware** made during the reign of Louis XIV. Finally, on the top floor, you'll come to a distinguished collection of historic scientific instruments, a small selection of arms and armour, plus sections on geology, fossils, ethnology and Oriental arts.

The Asian selection was boosted by the opening, in 1996, of the **Ivy Wu Gallery**, displaying the arts of China, Korea and Japan in a highly informative way. Look out for a splendid sixteenth-century Chinese throne and Buddhist art from each of the three civilizations.

THE UNIVERSITY

Map 3, G4.

Immediately alongside the Royal Museum is the earliest surviving part of the **University of Edinburgh**, variously referred to as **Old College** or Old Quad, although nowadays it houses only a few university departments; the main campus colonizes the streets and squares to the south.

The Old College was designed by Robert Adam, but built after his death in a considerably modified form by William Playfair (1789–1857), one of Edinburgh's greatest architects. Playfair built just one of Adam's two quadrangles (the dome was not added until 1879) and his magnificent **Upper Library** is now mostly used for ceremonial occasions.

THE UNIVERSITY

Darnley's murder

In January 1567, Lord Darnley, who had contracted smallpox, was brought to a church known as Kirk o'Field, close to what is now the quadrangle of Old College, in order to ensure that he did not infect his infant son in Holyrood. On the night of February 9, the building was destroyed by a huge explosion and the body of Darnley was found in the grounds outside. There were no signs of his body having been in an explosion: examination showed that he had been strangled. Mary, Queen of Scots, who had visited her husband on the evening in question and was later seen walking up Blackfriars Wynd, is generally considered to have been implicated in the murder. Whether such allegations are true, Mary was by then involved with the Earl of Bothwell, who was almost certainly responsible for the deed. After his arrest and suspiciously speedy acquittal, Bothwell abducted Mary on her way from Stirling to Linlithgow, divorced his own wife and married the queen on May 15, 1567. Within a month Mary had surrendered to the enraged nobles of Scotland: Bothwell fled to Orkney and then Norway, where he died in captivity eleven years later.

The Talbot Rice Art Gallery

Map 3, G4. Tues–Sat noon–5pm; free.

The **Talbot Rice Art Gallery**, housed in the Old College, includes many splendid seventeenth-century works from the Low Countries, with Teniers, Steen and van de Velde well represented. There are also some outstanding bronzes, notably the *Anatomical Horse* by an unknown Italian sculptor of the High Renaissance, and *Cain Killing Abel* by the Dutch Mannerist Adrian de Vries. The gallery also puts on regular exhibitions drawn from the University's substantial collection.

THE NEW TOWN

he **New Town**, itself well over two hundred years old, stands in total contrast to the Old Town: the layout is symmetrical, the streets broad and straight, and most of the buildings are Neoclassical. Originally intended to be residential, the entire area, right down to the names of its streets, is something of a celebration of the Union, which was then generally regarded as a proud development in Scotland's history. Today the New Town is the bustling hub of the city's professional, commercial and business life, dominated by shops, banks and offices.

The existence of the New Town is chiefly due to the vision of **George Drummond**, who made schemes for the expansion of the city soon after becoming Lord Provost in 1725. Work began on the draining of the Nor' Loch below the castle in 1759, a job that was to last some sixty years. The North Bridge, linking the Old Town with the port of Leith, was built between 1763 and 1772 and, in 1766, following a public competition, a plan for the New Town by a 20-year-old architect, **James Craig**, was chosen. Its gridiron pattern was perfectly matched to the site: the central **George Street**, flanked by showpiece squares, was laid out along the main ridge, with the parallel **Princes Street** and **Queen Street** on either side below, and two smaller streets,

Thistle Street and Rose Street in between the three major thoroughfares to provide coach houses, artisans' dwellings and shops. Princes and Queen streets were built up on one side only, so as not to block the spectacular views of the Old Town and Fife. Architects were accordingly afforded a wonderful opportunity to play with vistas and spatial relationships, particularly well exploited by Robert Adam, who contributed extensively to the later phases of the work. The First New Town, as the area covered by Craig's plan came to be known, received a whole series of extensions in the first few decades of the nineteenth century, all in harmony with the Neoclassical style.

In many ways, the layout of the New Town is its own most remarkable sight, an extraordinary grouping of squares, circuses, terraces, crescents and parks, with a few set pieces such as **Register House**, the north frontage of **Charlotte Square** and the assemblage of curiosities on and around **Calton Hill**. However, it also contains an assortment of Victorian additions, notably the **Scott Monument**, as well as three of the city's most important public collections – the **National Gallery of Scotland**, the **Scottish National Portrait Gallery** and the **Scottish National Gallery of Modern Art**.

On the northern edge of the New Town is one of Edinburgh's greatest features – the **Royal Botanic Garden**, an oasis of calm in a busy city.

PRINCES STREET

Map 4, I6.

Although only allocated a subsidiary role in the original plan of the New Town, **Princes Street** had developed into Edinburgh's principal thoroughfare by the middle of the last century, a role it has retained ever since. Its unobstructed views across to the castle and the Old Town are undeniably magnificent. Indeed, without the views, Princes Street would lose much of its appeal; its northern side, dominated by ugly department stores, is almost always crowded with shoppers, and few of the original eighteenth-century buildings remain.

It was the coming of the railway, which follows a parallel course to the south, that ensured Princes Street's rise to prominence. The tracks are well concealed at the far end of the sunken **gardens** that replaced the Nor' Loch, which provide ample space to relax or picnic during the summer. Thomas De Quincey (1785–1859), author of the classic account of drug addiction, *Confessions of an English Opium Eater* (published in 1821), spent the last thirty years of his life in Edinburgh and is buried in the graveyard of **St Cuthbert's Church**, beneath the castle at the western end of the gardens.

The East End

Map 4, K5.

Register House (Mon–Fri 10am–4pm; free), Princes Street's most distinguished building, stands at its extreme northeastern corner, framing the perspective down North Bridge, and providing a good visual link between the Old and New towns. Unfortunately, the majesty of the setting is marred by the **St James Centre** to the rear, a covered shopping arcade now regarded as the city's worst ever planning blunder. Register House was designed in the 1770s by Robert Adam to hold Scotland's historic records, a function it has maintained ever since. Its exterior is a model of restrained Neoclassicism; the interior, centred on a glorious Roman rotunda, has a dome lavishly decorated with plasterwork and antique-style medallions.

> **For a review of *The Balmoral* and other good places
> to stay in the New Town see p.99.**

Opposite is one of the few buildings on the south side of Princes Street, the **North British Hotel** or "NB" as it is popularly known, despite its redesignation as *The Balmoral* in a gesture of political correctness by its owners: North Britain was an alternative name for Scotland throughout the eighteenth and nineteenth centuries, and is regarded by Scots as an affront. Among the most luxurious hotels in the city, it has always been associated with the railway, and the timepiece on its bulky clock tower is always kept two minutes fast in order to encourage passengers to hurry to catch their trains. Alongside the hotel, the **Waverley Market** is a sensitive modern redevelopment that carefully avoided repeating the mistakes of the St James Centre. Its roof makes an excellent open-air piazza, a favourite haunt of street theatre groups and other performing artists during the Festival.

The Scott Monument and the Royal Scottish Academy

Map 4, H7.

Facing the Victorian shopping emporium Jenners (see p.177), and set within East Princes Street Gardens, the 200-foot-high **Scott Monument** (April–Sept 9am–6pm; Oct–March 9am–3pm; £1.50) was erected by public subscription in memory of the writer within a few years of his death. The largest monument in the world to a writer, its magisterial, spire-like design is due to George Meikle Kemp, a carpenter and joiner whose only building this is; while it was still under construction, he stumbled into a canal one foggy evening and drowned. The architecture is closely modelled on Scott's beloved Melrose Abbey, while the rich sculptural decoration shows 16 Scottish writers and 64 characters from the *Waverley* novels. Underneath the archway is a **statue** of Scott with his deerhound Maida, carved from a thirty-ton block of Carrara marble.

The monument's blackened condition is a pity, and it was recently hidden under shrouds for two years while studies were carried out as to the possibility of cleaning it by sandblasting, a technique successfully applied to many of Edinburgh's other historic buildings. This exercise divided professional opinion, some believing the monument to be too slender to stand up to the treatment. Eventually, it was decided that cleaning would not go ahead. The Scott Monument is closed in October 1997 for a year.

The Princes Street Gardens are bisected by the **Mound**, which provides a road link between the Old and New towns. Its name is an accurate description: it was formed in the 1780s by dumping piles of earth brought from the New Town's building plots. At the foot of the Mound, Playfair's **Royal Scottish Academy**, or RSA (Mon–Sat 10am–5pm, Sun 2–5pm; price varies), is a Grecian-style Doric temple used somewhat infrequently for temporary exhibitions during the year, notably for the RSA annual exhibition held from April to July.

Despite being one of the Neoclassical buildings which helped the city earn its tag of "Athens of the North", the RSA has declined into a bad state of repair and is now used only sporadically, the highlight being its annual exhibition held from April to July. This has led to talk of a possible merger with the National Gallery and even of closure. The problem has been exacerbated by the unedifying state of the building's exterior, where efforts to discourage its use as a public toilet have so far been unsuccessful. Playfair's Greek columns may now suffer the indignity of being joined together by railings. From a distance, though, the RSA still looks wonderful, the columned facade appearing most imposing from Hanover Street on the opposite side of Princes Street.

THE NATIONAL GALLERY OF SCOTLAND

Map 4, H8. Mon–Sat 10am–5pm, Sun 2–5pm; free.

To the rear of the Royal Scottish Academy, the **National Gallery of Scotland** is another Playfair construction, built in the 1840s and now housing a choice display of paintings, many of which belong to the Duke of Sutherland. The knowledgeable staff wear tartan trousers, one of a series of innovations introduced by the flamboyant English director, Timothy Clifford. A few years ago, and more controversially, the original Playfair rooms on the ground floor were restored to their 1840s appearance, with the pictures hung closely together, often on two levels, and intermingled with sculptures and *objets d'art* to produce a deliberately cluttered effect (some lesser works, which would otherwise languish in the vaults, are a good 15ft up). Two small, late nineteenth-century works in Room 12 – one anonymous, the other by A.E. Moffat – show the gallery as it was, with paintings stacked up even higher than at present.

Though individual works are frequently rearranged and well-known works are often out on loan, the layout is broadly chronological, starting in the upper rooms above the entrance, and continuing clockwise around the ground floor. The upper part of the rear extension is devoted to smaller panels of the eighteenth and nineteenth centuries, while the basement contains the majority of the Scottish collection.

Early Netherlandish and German works

Among the gallery's most valuable treasures are the *Trinity Panels*, the remaining parts of the only surviving pre-Reformation altarpiece made for a Scottish church. Painted by **Hugo van der Goes** in the mid-fifteenth century, they were commissioned for the Holy Trinity Collegiate Church by its provost Edward Bonkil, who appears in company of organ-playing angels in the finest and best preserved of the four panels. On the reverse sides are portraits of James III, his son (the future James IV) and Queen Margaret of Denmark. Their feebly characterized heads were modelled from life by an unknown local painter after the altar had been shipped to Edinburgh.

Of the later Netherlandish works, **Gerard David** is represented by the touchingly anecdotal *Three Legends of St Nicholas*, while the *Portrait of a Notary* by **Quentin Massys** is an excellent early example of northern European assimilation of the forms and techniques of the Italian Renaissance. Many of his German contemporaries developed their own variations on this style, among them **Cranach**, by whom there is a splendidly erotic *Venus and Cupid*, and **Holbein**, whose *Allegory of the Old and New Testaments* is a Protestant tract painted for an English patron.

The Italian Renaissance

The Italian section includes a wonderful array of **Renaissance** masterpieces, *The Virgin Adoring the Child*, a beautiful composition set against a ruined architectural background shown in strict perspective: although known to have been painted in the workshop of the great Florentine sculptor **Andrea del Verrocchio**, its authorship remains a mystery. Equally graceful are the three works by **Raphael**, particularly *The Bridgewater Madonna* and the tondo of *The Holy Family with a Palm Tree*, whose striking luminosity has been revealed after recent restoration.

Of the four mythological scenes by **Titian**, the allegorical *Three Ages of Man* is one of the most accomplished compositions of his early period, while the later *Venus Anadyomene* ranks among the great nudes of Western art, notwithstanding its rough state of preservation. The companion pair of *Diana and Acteon* and *Diana and Calisto*, painted for Philip II of Spain, show the almost impressionistic freedom of his late style. **Bassano**'s truly regal *Adoration of the Kings*, a dramatic altarpiece of *The Descent from the Cross* by **Tintoretto**, and several other works by **Veronese**, complete a fine Venetian collection.

The seventeenth century

Among the seventeenth-century works is the gallery's most important sculpture, **Bernini**'s *Bust of Monsignor Carlo Antonio dal Pozzo*. **El Greco**'s *A Fable*, painted during his early years in Italy, is a mysterious subject whose exact meaning is unclear, while *The Saviour of the World* is a typically intense, visionary image from his mature years in Spain. Indigenous Spanish art is represented by **Velázquez**'s *An Old Woman Cooking Eggs*, an astonishingly assured work for a lad of 19, and by **Zurbarán**'s *The Immaculate Conception*, part of his ambitious decorative scheme of the Carthusian monastery in Jerez. There are two small copper panels by the short-lived but enormously influential Rome-based German painter **Adam Elsheimer**; of these, *Il Contento*, showing Jupiter's descent to Earth to punish the ungodly, is a *tour de force* of technical precision.

A series of *The Seven Sacraments* by **Poussin** is displayed in its own room. Based on the artist's own extensive research into biblical times, the set marks the first attempt to portray scenes from the life of Jesus and the early Christians in an historically authentic manner. The result is profoundly touching, with a myriad of imaginative and subtle details. **Claude**, who likewise left France to live in Rome, is represented by his largest canvas, *Landscape with Apollo, the Muses and a River God*, which radiates his characteristically idealized vision of Classical antiquity.

As for Poussin and Claude's contemporaries in the Low Countries, **Rubens**' *The Feast of Herod* is an archetypal example of his grand manner, in which the gory subject matter is overshadowed by the depiction of the delights of the table. Like all his large works, it was executed with extensive studio assistance, whereas the three small sketches, including the highly finished *Adoration of the Shepherds*, are all from his own hand. The trio of large upright canvases by **Van Dyck** date from his early Genoese period; of these, *The Lomellini Family* shows his mastery at creating a definitive dynastic image.

Among the four canvases by **Rembrandt** is a poignant *Self-Portrait Aged 51*, and the ripely suggestive *Woman in Bed*, which probably represents the biblical figure of Sarah on her wedding night, waiting for her husband Tobias to put the devil to flight. *Christ in the House of Martha and Mary* is the largest and probably the earliest of the thirty or so surviving paintings of **Vermeer**; as the only one with a religious subject, it inspired a notorious series of forgeries by Han van Meegeren. By **Hals** are a typical pair of portraits plus a brilliant caricature, *Verdonck*. There's also an excellent cross section of the specialist Dutch painters of the age, highlights being the mischievous *School for Boys and Girls* by **Jan Steen**, and the strangely haunting *Interior of the Church of St Bavo in Haarlem* by **Pieter Saenredam**, one of the gallery's most expensive purchases.

The eighteenth and nineteenth centuries

Of the large-scale eighteenth-century works, **Tiepolo**'s *The Finding of Moses*, a gloriously bravura fantasy, stands out. Other decorative compositions of the same period are **Goya**'s *The Doctor*, a cartoon for a tapestry design, and the three large pastoral scenes by **Boucher**. However, the gems of the French section are the smaller panels, in particular **Watteau**'s *Fêtes Vénitiennes*, an effervescent Rococo idyll, and **Chardin**'s *Vase of Flowers*, a copybook example of still-life painting. One of the gallery's most recent major purchases is **Canova**'s statue *The Three Graces* – saved at the last minute from the hands of the Getty Museum in California.

There's also a superb group of Impressionist and Post-Impressionist masterpieces, including a particularly good cross section of the works of **Degas**, three outstanding examples of **Gauguin**, set respectively in Brittany, Martinique and Tahiti, and **Cézanne**'s *The Tall Trees* – a clear forerunner of modern abstraction.

English and American paintings

Surprisingly, the gallery has relatively few **English** paintings, but those here are impressive. **Hogarth**'s *Sarah Malcolm*, painted in Newgate Prison the day the murderess was executed, once belonged to Horace Walpole, who also commissioned **Reynolds**' *The Ladies Waldegrave*, a group portrait of his three great-nieces. **Gainsborough**'s *The Honourable Mrs Graham* is one of his most memorable society portraits, while **Constable** himself described *Dedham Vale* as being "perhaps my best". There are two prime Roman views by **Turner**, by whom the gallery owns a wonderful array of watercolours, displayed each January.

Even more unexpected than the scarcity of English works is the presence of some exceptional **American** canvases:

Benjamin West's Romantic fantasy, *King Alexander III Rescued from a Stag*; **John Singer Sargent**'s virtuosic *Lady Agnew of Lochnaw*; and **Frederic Edwin Church**'s *View of Niagara Falls from the American Side*. The last, having been kept in store for decades, was put back on display when the "rediscovery" of the artist in the late 1970s prompted astronomical bids from American museums keen to acquire the only work by the artist owned by a European gallery.

Scottish art

On the face of it, the gallery's **Scottish** collection, which shows the entire gamut of Scottish painting from seventeenth-century portraiture to the Arts and Crafts movement, is something of an anticlimax. There are, however, some important works – **Gavin Hamilton**'s *Achilles Mourning the Death of Patroclus*, for example, painted in Rome, is an unquestionably arresting image. **Allan Ramsay**, who became court painter to George III, is represented by his intimate *The Artist's Second Wife* and *Jean-Jacques Rousseau*, in which the philosopher is shown in Armenian costume.

Of **Sir Henry Raeburn**'s large portraits, note *Sir John Sinclair* and *Colonel Alistair MacDonell of Glengarry*, both of whom are shown in full Highland dress. Raeburn's technical mastery was equally sure when working on a small scale, as shown in one of the gallery's most popular pictures, *The Rev Robert Walker Skating on Duddingston Loch*.

Other Scottish painters represented include the versatile **Sir David Wilkie**, whose huge history painting, *Sir David Baird Discovering the Body of Sultan Tippo Saib*, is in marked contrast to the early documentary and genre scenes displayed in the basement, and **Alexander Nasmyth**, whose tendency to gild the lily can be seen in his *View of Tantallon*

Castle and the Bass Rock, where the dramatic scenery is further spiced up by the inclusion of a shipwreck.

GEORGE STREET AND CHARLOTTE SQUARE

Map 4, B7.

Just north and parallel to Princes Street is **George Street**, the city's chief financial thoroughfare and the least prepossessing of the main streets of the First New Town. At its eastern end lies **St Andrew Square**, in the middle of which is the Melville Monument, a statue of Lord Melville, Pitt the Younger's Navy Treasurer. On the eastern side of the square stands a handsome eighteenth-century town mansion, designed by Sir William Chambers and headquarters of the Royal Bank of Scotland since 1825. The palatial mid-nineteenth-century banking hall epitomizes the success of the New Town. On the south side of the street, the oval-shaped church of **St Andrew** (now known as St Andrew and St George) is chiefly famous as the scene of the 1843 Disruption led by Thomas Chalmers, which split the Church of Scotland in two. Famous visitors to George Street have included Percy Bysshe Shelley, who stayed at no. 60 with the 16-year-old Harriet Westbrook during the summer of 1811, and Charles Dickens who gave a number of readings of his works in the Assembly Rooms in the 1840s and 1850s.

At the western end of the street, **Charlotte Square** was designed by Robert Adam in 1791, a year before his death. For the most part, his plans were faithfully implemented, an exception being the domed and porticoed church of St George, which was simplified on grounds of expense. Its interior was gutted in the 1960s and refurbished as **West Register House**; like its counterpart at the opposite end of Princes Street, it features changing documentary exhibitions (Mon–Fri 10am–4pm; free).

The Georgian House

Map 4, B6.

The north side of the square has become the most exclusive address in the city. No. 6 is the official residence of the Secretary of State for Scotland, while the upper storeys of no. 7 are the home of the Moderator of the General Assembly, the annually elected leader of the Church of Scotland. Restored by the NTS, the lower floors are open to the public under the name of the **Georgian House** (April–Oct Mon–Sat 10am–5pm, Sun 2–5pm; £4), whose contents give a good idea of what the house must have looked like during the period of the first owner, the head of the clan Lamont. The rooms are decked out in period furniture, including a working barrel organ which plays a selection of Scottish airs, and hung with fine paintings, including portraits by Ramsay and Raeburn, seventeenth-century Dutch cabinet pictures, and a beautiful *Marriage of the Virgin* by El Greco's teacher, the Italian miniaturist Giulio Clovio. In the basement are the original wine cellar, lined with roughly made bins, and a kitchen, complete with an open fire for roasting and a separate oven for baking; video reconstructions of life below and above stairs are shown in a nearby room.

QUEEN STREET

Map 4, C5.

Queen Street, the last of the three main streets of the First New Town, is bordered to the north by gardens, and commands sweeping views across to Fife. Much the best preserved of the area's three main streets, its principal attraction is its excellent gallery-cum-museum.

The Scottish National Portrait Gallery

Map 4, J3. Mon–Sat 10am–5pm, Sun 2–5pm; free.

At the far eastern end of Queen Street stands the **Scottish National Portrait Gallery.** The building is itself a fascinating period piece, its red sandstone exterior, modelled on the Doge's Palace in Venice, encrusted with statues of famous Scots – a theme taken up in the entrance hall, which has a mosaic-like frieze procession by William Hole of great figures from Scotland's past, with heroic murals by the same artist of stirring episodes from the nation's history adorning the balcony above. The Museum of Antiquities used to be housed here too, but the exhibits have now moved to the new Royal Museum of Scotland annexe, due to open in November 1998 (see p.52).

The Stewart Exhibition

On the ground floor of the western wing, an exhibition on the **Stewart dynasty** traces the history of the family from its origins as stewards (hence the name) to medieval royalty, via its zenith under James VI, who engineered the union with England, to its final demise under Bonnie Prince Charlie.

From the early periods, look out for two superb artefacts from the reign of Robert the Bruce, the **Kames Brooch** and the **Bute Mazer** (a large wooden bowl). An excellent collection of Mary, Queen of Scots memorabilia includes her **Penicuik Jewels** and a portrait by Rowland Lockey. The reign of Charles I is represented by several outstanding paintings by Flemish artists including **Daniel Mytens** and **Alexander Keirinocx**, and there are fine official portraits of the later Stewart monarchs and members of their entourage. Mementos of the Young Pretender include the ornate backsword and silver-mounted shield with which he fought at Culloden, and a **canteen** he left abandoned on the battlefield.

The Portrait Gallery

The floors above the Stewart exhibition are devoted to portraits, accompanied by potted biographies, of famous Scots – a definition stretched to include anyone with the slightest Scottish connection. From the seventeenth century, there's an excellent Van Dyck portrait of Charles Seton, second Earl of Dunfermline, and the tartan-clad Lord Mungo Murray, who died in the disastrous attempt to establish a Scottish colony in Panama. Eighteenth-century highlights include portraits of the philosopher-historian David Hume by Allan Ramsay, the poet Robert Burns by his friend Alexander Nasmyth, and a varied group by Raeburn: subjects include Sir Walter Scott, the fiddler Niel Gow, and the artist himself. The star portrait from the nineteenth century is that of physician Sir Alexander Morison by his patient, the mad painter **Richard Dadd** – Edinburgh's fishing port of Newhaven is in the background. Twentieth-century portraits include a very angular Alec Douglas-Home, briefly prime minister in the 1960s, the stern figure of union leader Mick McGahey, soccer star Danny McGrain (in a kilt) and film-maker Bill Forsyth.

NORTHERN NEW TOWN

Map 4, L1.

The Northern New Town was the earliest extension to the First New Town, begun in 1801, and today roughly covers the area north of Queen Street between India Street to the west and Broughton Street to the east and as far as Fettes Row to the north. This has survived in far better shape than its predecessor: with the exception of one street, almost all of it is intact, and it has managed to preserve its predominantly residential character.

NORTHERN NEW TOWN

One of the area's most intriguing buildings is the Neo-Norman **Mansfield Place Church**, on the corner of Broughton and East London streets, designed in the late nineteenth century for the strange, now defunct Catholic Apostolic sect. Having lain redundant and neglected for three decades, it has suddenly acquired cult status, its preservation the current obsession of local conservation groups. The chief reason for this is its cycle of murals by the Dublin-born Phoebe Traquair, a leading light in the Scottish Arts and Crafts movement. She laboured for eight years on this decorative scheme, which has all the freshness and luminosity of a medieval manuscript, but desperately needs a thorough restoration to avert its already alarming decay. Interest in the murals was revived in 1993 when the church was opened to the public for the summer. The main body of the church, whose basement is used regularly as a nightclub – *Café Graffiti* (see p.150) – will in the future house a centre for Scottish voluntary groups.

Dean Village and Stockbridge

Work began on the western end of the New Town in 1822, in a small area of land north of Charlotte Square and west of George Street. Instead of the straight lines of the earlier sections, there were now the gracious curves of **Randolph Crescent**, **Ainslie Place** and the magnificent twelve-sided **Moray Place**, designed by the vainglorious James Gillespie Graham who described himself, with no authority to do so, as "architect in Scotland to the Prince Regent". Round the corner from Randolph Crescent, the four-arched **Dean Bridge**, a bravura feat of 1830s engineering by Thomas Telford, carries the main road high above Edinburgh's placid little river, the **Water of Leith**. Down to the left lies

Dean Village (Map 2, A5), an old milling community that is one of central Edinburgh's most picturesque yet oddest corners, its atmosphere of terminal decay arrested by the conversion of some of the mills into chic flats. The riverside path into Stockbridge passes **St Bernard's Well**, a pump room covered by a mock-Roman temple. Commissioned in 1788 by Lord Gardenstone to draw mineral waters from the Water of Leith, it has been recently restored, and is occasionally open (phone ℭ445 7367 for details).

Stockbridge (Map 2, B2), which straddles both sides of the Water of Leith on the other side of Dean Bridge, is another old village which has retained its distinctive identity, in spite of its absorption into the Georgian face of the New Town, and is particularly renowned for its antique shops and "alternative" outlets. The residential upper streets on the far side of the river were developed by Sir Henry Raeburn, who named the finest of them **Ann Street**, which after Charlotte Square is the most prestigious address in Edinburgh (writers Thomas De Quincey and J.M. Ballantyne were residents); alone among New Town streets, its houses each have a front garden.

The Scottish National Gallery of Modern Art

Map 2, A5. Mon–Sat 10am–5pm, Sun 2–5pm; free.

Set in spacious wooded grounds at the far northwestern fringe of the New Town, about ten minutes' walk from either the cathedral or Dean Village, the **Scottish National Gallery of Modern Art** was established in 1959 as the first collection in Britain devoted solely to twentieth-century painting and sculpture. The grounds serve as a sculpture park, featuring works by Jacob Epstein, Henry Moore, Barbara Hepworth and the Constructivist creations of the Edinburgh-born Eduardo Paolozzi, soon to be

THE SCOTTISH NATIONAL GALLERY OF MODERN ART |

honoured with his own museum in the massive Dean Centre on the opposite side of Belford Road. Inside, the display space is divided between temporary loan exhibitions and selections from the gallery's own holdings; the latter are arranged thematically, but are almost constantly moved around. What you get to see at any particular time is therefore a matter of chance, though the most important works are nearly always on view.

French painters are particularly well represented, beginning with **Bonnard**'s *Lane at Vernonnet* and **Vuillard**'s jewel-like *Two Seamstresses*, and by a few examples of the Fauves, notably **Matisse**'s *The Painting Lesson* and **Derain**'s dazzlingly brilliant *Collioure*; there's also a fine group of late canvases by **Leger**, notably *The Constructors*. Among some striking examples of German Expressionism are **Kirchner**'s *Japanese Theatre*, **Feininger**'s *Gelmeroda III*, and a wonderfully soulful wooden sculpture of a woman by **Barlach** entitled *The Terrible Year, 1937*. Highlights of the Surrealist section are **Magritte**'s haunting *Black Flag*, **Miró**'s seminal *Composition* and **Giacometti**'s repulsive *Woman with her Throat Cut*, while Cubism is represented by **Picasso**'s *Soles* and **Braque**'s *Candlestick*.

Of works by American artists, **Roy Lichtenstein**'s *In the Car* is a fine example of his Pop Art style, while **Duane Hanson**'s fibreglass *Tourists* is typically cruel. English artists on show include Sickert, Nicholson, Spencer, Freud and Hockney, but, as you'd expect, considerably more space is allocated to Scottish artists. Of particular note are the so-called Colourists – **S.J. Peploe, J.D. Fergusson, Francis Cadell** and **George Leslie Hunter** – whose works are attracting fancy prices on the art market, as well as ever-growing posthumous critical acclaim. Although they did not form a recognizable school, they all worked in France and displayed considerable French influence in their warm, bright palettes.

The gallery also shows works by many contemporary Scots, among them **John Bellany**, a portraitist of striking originality, and the poet-artist-gardener **Ian Hamilton Finlay**.

THE ROYAL BOTANIC GARDEN

Map 2, C1. Daily: March, April, Sept & Oct 10am–6pm; May–Aug 10am–8pm; Nov–Feb 10am–4pm; free.

Just beyond the northern boundaries of the New Town, with entrances on Inverleith Row and Arboretum Place, is the seventy-acre site of the **Royal Botanic Garden** particularly renowned for the **rhododendrons**, which blaze out in a glorious patchwork of colours in April and May. In the heart of the grounds a group of hothouses designated the **Glasshouse Experience** displays orchids, giant Amazonian water lilies, and a 200-year-old West Indian palm tree, the latter being in the elegant 1850s glass-topped Palm House. Many of the most exotic plants were brought to Edinburgh by the aptly named George Forrest, who made seven expeditions to southwestern China between 1904 and 1932. There is also a major new Chinese-style garden, featuring a pavilion, waterfall and the world's biggest collection of Chinese wild plants outside China.

The *Terrace Café* at the Royal Botanic Gardens offers stunning views of the Royal Mile (see p.121).

At the highest point of the gardens is **Inverleith House**, built in 1774, formerly used for the Gallery of Modern Art, and now used for exhibitions. From the lawn to the south of the house, just next to a handy café, there are marvellous views across to the Old Town, one of the best places in the city to see the whole of the Royal Mile. There is now a well-stocked gift and plant shop by the western entrance.

THE ROYAL BOTANIC GARDEN

CALTON

Map 7.

Of the various extensions to the New Town, the most intriguing is **Calton**, which branches out from the eastern end of Princes Street and encircles a volcanic hill. For years the centre of a thriving gay scene (see p.164), it is an area of extraordinary showpiece architecture, dating from the time of the Napoleonic Wars or just after.

Waterloo Place forms a ceremonial way from Princes Street to Calton Hill. On its southern side is the sombre and overgrown **Old Calton Burial Ground**, in which you can see Robert Adam's plain, cylindrical memorial to David Hume and a monument, complete with a statue of Abraham Lincoln, to the Scots who died in the American Civil War. Hard up against the cemetery's eastern wall, perched above a sheer rockface, is a picturesque castellated building which many visitors arriving at Waverley Station below imagine to be Edinburgh Castle itself. In fact, it's the only surviving part of the **Calton Jail**, once Edinburgh's main prison. Next door is the massive **St Andrew's House**, built in the 1930s to house civil servants.

Further on, set majestically in a confined site below Calton Hill, is one of Edinburgh's greatest buildings, the Grecian **Old Royal High School**. Previously in the Old Town, Edinburgh's oldest school is now a frontrunner in the contest to be Scotland's new parliament building former *alma mater* to, among others, Robert Adam, Walter Scott, and Alexander Graham Bell, who was given this new house by Thomas Hamilton, himself an old boy. Across the road, Hamilton also built the **Burns Monument**, a circular Corinthian temple modelled on the Monument to Lysicrates in Athens, as a memorial to the national bard.

Robert Louis Stevenson reckoned that **Calton Hill** was the best place to view Edinburgh, "since you can see the castle, which you lose from the castle, and Arthur's Seat, which you cannot see from Arthur's Seat". Though the panoramas from ground level are spectacular enough, those from the top of the **Nelson Monument** (April–Sept Mon 1–6pm, Tues–Sat 10am–6pm; Oct–March Mon–Sat 10am–3pm; £1.50) are even better. Begun just two years after Nelson's death at Trafalgar, this is one of Edinburgh's oddest buildings, resembling a gigantic spyglass.

Alongside, the **National Monument** was begun in 1822 by Playfair to plans by the English architect Charles Cockerell. Had it been completed, it would have been a reasonably accurate replica of the Parthenon, but funds ran out with only twelve columns built. Various later schemes to finish it similarly foundered, earning it the nickname "Edinburgh's Disgrace". At the opposite side of the hill, the grandeur of Playfair's Classical **Monument to Dugald Stewart** seems totally disproportionate to the stature of the man it commemorates: a now-forgotten professor of philosophy at the University.

Playfair also built the **City Observatory** for his uncle, the mathematician and astronomer John Playfair, whom he honoured in the cenotaph outside. Because of pollution and the advent of street lighting, which impaired views of the stars, the observatory proper had to be relocated to Blackford Hill before the end of the century, though the equipment here continues to be used by students. The small domed pavilion at the northeastern corner, an addition of the 1890s, now houses the **Edinburgh Experience** (April–June, Sept & Oct Mon–Fri 2–5pm, Sat & Sun 10.30am–5pm; July & Aug daily 10.30am–5pm; £2), a twenty minute 3-D show on the city's history viewed through special glasses. At the opposite end of the complex is the **Old Observatory**, one of the few surviving buildings by James Craig, designer of the New Town.

CALTON |

THE
SUBURBS

There are a number of places worth visiting in the belt of land on the south side of the **Firth of Forth**, all of them easily reached by public transport. An hour's boat trip from **South Queensferry** takes you past the magestic **Forth Rail Bridge** and **Hopetoun House**, an eighteenth-century stately home with hugely impressive grounds, to **Inchcolm Island** where a ruined medieval abbey awaits. At the western edge of Edinburgh lies the small community of **Dalmeny** and **Cramond**, an attractive village with a history going back to Roman times; a mile or so to the east stands **Lauriston Castle**, a country house with expansive grounds looking out to the Forth, and home to a quirky assortment of antiques. Further east lie the ports of **Newhaven**, once the home of Edinburgh's fishing market, and **Leith**, a former dock area now rejuvenated by offices and a seemingly ever-expanding selection of bars and quality restaurants. Finally, **Portobello**, at the eastern edge of the city, until recently a busy seaside resort, has a long promenade that offers excellent walks.

SOUTH QUEENSFERRY AND AROUND

Map 1, B3.

South Queensferry is a compact little town that was used by St Margaret as a crossing point for her frequent trips between her palaces in Edinburgh and Dunfermline. **High Street**, squeezed into the narrow gap between the seashore and the hillside above, is lined by a picturesque array of old buildings, among them an unusual two-tiered row of shops, the roofs of the lower level serving as the walkway for the upper storey. The small **museum** at 53 High Street (Mon & Thurs–Sat 10am–1pm & 2.15–5pm, Sun 2–5pm; free) contains relics of the town's history and the building of its two bridges.

Everything in South Queensferry is overshadowed, quite literally, by the two great bridges, each about a mile and a half in length, which traverse the Firth of Forth at its narrowest point. The cantilevered **Forth Rail Bridge**, built from 1883 to 1890 by Sir John Fowler and Benjamin Baker, ranks among the supreme achievements of Victorian engineering. Some 50,000 tons of steel were used in the construction of a design that manages to exude grace as well as might. Derived from American models, the suspension format chosen for the **Forth Road Bridge** makes a perfect complement to the older structure. Erected between 1958 and 1964, it finally killed off the 900-year-old ferry, and now attracts a heavy volume of traffic. It's well worth walking across its footpath to Fife for the tremendous views of the Rail Bridge.

Hopetoun House

Map 1, A3. Daily: April–Oct 10am–6.30pm; **house and grounds** £4.50, **grounds only** £2.50.

One of Scotland's grandest stately homes, **Hopetoun House**, lies immediately beyond the western edge of South

Queensferry. The original house was built at the turn of the eighteenth century for the first Earl of Hopetoun by Sir William Bruce, the architect of Holyroodhouse (see p.39). A couple of decades later, William Adam carried out an enormous extension, engulfing the house in a curvaceous main facade and two projecting wings – superb facsimiles of Roman Baroque pomp and swagger.

> **The grounds of Hopetoun House are used for concerts during the summer; phone ©0131 331 2451 for details.**

The scale and lavishness of the Adam **interiors**, most of whose decoration was carried out after the architect's death by his sons, make for a stark contrast with the intimacy of those designed by Bruce. Particularly impressive are the Red and Yellow **Drawing Rooms**, with their splendid ceilings by the young Robert Adam. Among the house's furnishings are seventeenth-century tapestries, Meissen porcelain, and a distinguished collection of paintings, including portraits by Gainsborough, Ramsay and Raeburn. The grounds of Hopetoun House are also open, with magnificent walks along the banks of the Forth, and provide great opportunities for picnics. From the northwestern corner of the grounds, look upriver to the ship-like shape of the fifteenth-century **Blackness Castle**. Walking back towards the house you can see the only surviving feature of Bruce's design, the west face of the central section of the building.

Inchcolm

Map 1, C3.

The most enticing destination from South Queensferry's Hawes Pier (Easter, May & June Sat & Sun; daily July to mid-Sept; £6.50–8.95; ©331 4857) is the island of

Inchcolm, whose beautiful ruined **Abbey** (April–Sept Mon–Sat 9.30am–6.30pm, Sun 2–6.30pm; £2.30 though the cost of admission is included in your fee for the boat trip) was founded in 1123 by King Alexander I in gratitude for the hospitality he received from a hermit (whose cell survives at the northwestern corner of the island) when his ship was forced ashore in a storm. The best-preserved medieval monastic complex in Scotland, the abbey's surviving buildings date from the thirteenth to the fifteenth centuries, and include a splendid octagonal chapterhouse. Although the church is almost totally dilapidated, its tower can be ascended for a great aerial view of the island, which is populated by a variety of nesting birds and a colony of grey seals.

DALMENY

Map 1, B4.

In 1975, Edinburgh's boundaries were extended to include a number of towns and villages which were formerly part of West Lothian. Among them is **Dalmeny**, two miles west of Cramond, which can be reached directly from the city centre by bus (#43 Scottish Eastern) or train. Another option is to take the coastal path from Cramond, which passes through the estate of **Dalmeny House** (July & Aug Mon & Tues noon–5.30pm, Sun 1–5.30pm; £3.60), the seat of the Earls of Rosebery. Built in 1815 by the English architect William Wilkins, it was the first stately home in Scotland in the neo-Gothic style, vividly evoking Tudor architecture in its picturesque turreted roofline, and in its fan vaults and hammerbeam ceilings. The family portraits include one of the fourth Earl (who commissioned the house) by Raeburn, and of the fifth Earl (the last British prime minister to govern from the House of Lords) by Millais; there are also likenesses of other famous society figures by Reynolds, Gainsborough and

Lawrence. Among the furnishings are a set of tapestries made from cartoons by Goya, and the Rothschild Collection of eighteenth-century French furniture and *objets d'art*. There's also a fascinating collection of memorabilia of Napoleon Bonaparte – notably some items he used during his exile in St Helena – amassed by the fifth Earl, who wrote a biography of the French dictator.

Dalmeny **village** is a quiet community built around a spacious green. Its focal point is the mid-twelfth-century **St Cuthbert's Kirk**, a wonderful Norman church that has remained more or less intact. Although very weather-beaten, the south doorway is particularly notable for its illustrations of strange beasts. More vivaciously grotesque carvings can be seen inside on the chancel corbels and arch.

CRAMOND AND LAURISTON CASTLE

Map 1, C4.
Cramond is one of the city's most atmospheric – and poshest – old villages. The enduring image of this village is of step-gabled whitewashed houses rising uphill from the waterfront, though it also boasts the foundations of a Roman fort, a medieval bridge and tower house, and a church, inn and mansion, all from the seventeenth century. In December 1996, a wonderful Roman sculpture of a lioness devouring a man was discovered in the River Almond here: it is thought that it was simply thrown into the river after the departure of the Romans. The sculpture will eventually be displayed in one of the city's museums.

There are a number of interesting short walks in the area: across the causeway at low tide to the uninhabited (except for seabirds) **Cramond Island**; eastwards along the seafront towards the gasometers of Granton with sweeping views out to sea; and upstream along the River Almond past former mills and their adjoining cottages towards the six-teenth-century Old Cramond Brig. Each of these walks should take you around an hour each.

Lauriston Castle

Map 1, C4. Guided tours: mid-June to mid-Sept daily except Fri 11am–5pm; April to mid-June & mid-Sept to Oct daily except Fri 11am–1pm & 2–5pm; Nov–March Sat & Sun 2–4pm; £3. Bus #41 from the city centre.

Roughly five miles west of the city centre and a mile east of Cramond stands **Lauriston Castle**, a country mansion set in its own parkland overlooking the Firth of Forth. The original sixteenth-century tower house forms the centrepiece of what is otherwise a neo-Jacobean structure, which in 1902 became the retirement home of a prosperous local cabinet-maker. He decked out the interior with his private collection of furniture and antiques, some intriguing domestic features ranging from central heating and secondary glazing to an *en-suite* Edwardian bathroom incorporating a flushing toilet and a splendidly stur-dy bath-cum-shower and Flemish tapestries and ornaments made of Blue John from Derbyshire. Following the death in 1926 of the last private owners, Lauriston Castle was gifted to the nation and the interior has been left untouched.

Although well within the city boundaries, the castle is set on large grounds (daily 9am–dusk), including croquet lawns, offering wonderful views down to the Firth of Forth and across to Fife.

LEITH AND AROUND

Map 1, E4.

For several hundred years **Leith** was separate from Edinburgh. As Scotland's major east-coast port, it played a key role in the nation's history, even serving as the seat of government for a time, and in 1833 finally became a burgh in its own right. In 1920 it was incorporated into the capital, and in the decades that followed the area went into seemingly terminal decline: the population dropped dramatically, and much of its centre was ripped out, to be replaced by grim housing schemes.

The 1980s, however, saw an astonishing turnaround. Against all the odds, a couple of waterfront bistros proved enormously successful; competitors followed apace, and by the end of the decade the port had acquired what's arguably the best concentration of restaurants and pubs in Edinburgh. The surviving historic monuments were spruced up and a host of housing developments built or restored, a renaissance crowned by the completion of a vast new building for the Scottish Office. Nonetheless, away from the port's swanky waterfront bars and cafés, urban squalor, prostitution and poverty still exist, providing fertile material for the hugely successful novels of Irvine Welsh. Despite the fact that there is not a single shot of Leith in the film version of *Trainspotting*, it's done a lot to give Leith a cool reputation in certain circles.

For reviews of the best places to eat in Leith, see p.129; for the trendiest places to drink, see p.146.

To reach Leith from the city centre, take one of the many buses going down Leith Walk, near the top end of which is a statue of Sherlock Holmes, whose creator, Sir Arthur Conan Doyle, was born nearby. Otherwise, it's a brisk walk of around twenty minutes.

While you're most likely to come to Leith for the bars and restaurants, the area itself warrants exploration; though the shipbuilding yards have gone, it remains an active port with a rough-edged character. Most of the showpiece Neoclassical buildings lie on or near **The Shore**, the tenement-lined road along the final stretch of the Water of Leith, just before it disgorges into the Firth of Forth. Note the former **Town Hall**, on the parallel Constitution Street, now the headquarters of the local constabulary, immortalized in the tongue twister, "The Leith police dismisseth us"; the Classical **Trinity House** on Kirkgate, built in 1816, and the massive **Customs House** on Commercial Street. To the west of the town mall, set back from The Shore, is **Lamb's House**. Built as the home of the prosperous merchant Andro Lamb, this mansion was traditionally thought to be the first house visited by Mary, Queen of Scots on her arrival from France in 1561, though in fact it was not built until the start of the seventeenth century. Today it functions as an old people's day centre.

An area of predominantly flat parkland, **Leith Links**, lies just east of the police station. Documentary evidence suggests that The Links was a golf course in the fifteenth century, giving rise to Leith's claim to be regarded as the birthplace of the sport. Charles I played here and in 1744 its first written rules were drawn up at The Links, ten years before they were formalized in St Andrews.

Newhaven

Map 1, D4.

To the west of Leith lies the village of **Newhaven**, built by James IV at the start of the sixteenth century as an alternative shipbuilding centre to Leith: his massive warship, the *Michael*, capable of carrying 120 gunners, 300 mariners and 1000 troops, and said to have used up all the trees in Fife, was built here. The ship was never actually used and some of its timbers apparently ended up in Gladstone's Land (see p.21).

The harbour has also served as a ferry station and an important fishing centre, landing at the height of its success (in the 1860s) some six million oysters a year. Today, although a few boats still operate from here, the fish market is no more and the last of the colourfully dressed fishwives has long since retired. A variety of costumes and other memorabilia of the village's only industry can be found in the small **Newhaven Heritage Museum** (daily noon–5pm; free), a fascinating collection staffed by enthusiastic members of local fishing families.

Portobello

Map 1, F4. Bus #15, #26, #42 or #86 from the city centre.

Among Edinburgh's least-expected assets is its beach, most of which falls within **Portobello**, about three miles east of the centre of town. Founded in 1739 on wasteland between Leith and Musselburgh, the area was named after the naval victory of Puerto Bello in Panama. In Victorian times and even in the early part of this century, Portobello was a busy resort, known as "Brighton of the North". Today, in spite of a few tacky amusement arcades and a half-hearted funfair, it retains a certain faded charm, and a walk along the promenade is a pleasure at any time of the year.

For the best places to drink in Portobello, see p.148.

The streets running down to the beach are an interesting mishmash of Georgian and Victorian houses; the odd-looking **Tower** near the western end of the promenade was built in 1785 as a summer house, using stones from assorted demolished medieval houses, including, so tradition has it, the Mercat Cross, the old buildings of Edinburgh University and even parts of St Andrews Cathedral. Nearby

PORTOBELLO

in Bridge Street, a plaque marks the birthplace of music-hall giant **Sir Harry Lauder** (1870–1950), responsible for famously sentimental songs such as *Roamin' in the Gloamin* and *I Love a Lassie.*

DAY-TRIPS FROM EDINBURGH

T he site of several important events in Scotland's turbulent history are within easy reach of Edinburgh. To the west of the capital by the side of Linlithgow Loch lie the monumental ruins of **Linlithgow Palace**, birthplace of both James V and Mary, Queen of Scots. Scotland's famous queen was crowned in the Chapel Royal of **Stirling Castle**, slightly further to the north. Stirling's majestic and impressively restored castle was at the centre of the Scottish struggle for independence, culminating in 1314 when Robert the Bruce's army prevailed over the English enemy at the battle of Bannockburn.

To the east of Edinburgh are two smaller castles, **Tantallon Castle**, positioned dramatically on a headland surrounded on three sides by the Firth of Forth, and **Dirleton Castle**, which lies at the heart of a peaceful village. Both were residences of powerful families whose fluctuating fortunes saw control pass from Scottish to English hands and back again before eventually succumbing to Cromwell's marauding troops. Each has been a ruin since the middle of the seventeenth century.

Inland and to the south of Edinburgh, in the heart of the rich Midlothian countryside, are two rather different buildings, each noteworthy for its unique architecture: the stocky ruins of the fourteenth-century **Crichton Castle** and, just a few miles away, **Rosslyn Chapel**, with its extraordinary carvings, both religious and profoundly secular.

Apart from Crichton Castle, which lies around two miles west of the A68, these sites are all easily accessible by public transport. Regular trains run from Waverley Station to both Linlithgow and Stirling, while Tantallon, Roslin and Dirleton are all close to bus routes.

LINLITHGOW PALACE

Map 8. April–Sept Mon–Sat 9.30am–6.30pm, Sun 2–6.30pm; Oct–March Mon–Sat 9.30am–4.30pm, Sun 2–4.30pm; £2.30.

Linlithgow Palace is a splendid fifteenth-century ruin romantically set on the edge of Linlithgow Loch and associated with some of Scotland's best-known historical figures – including the ubiquitous Mary, Queen of Scots, who was born here in 1542. A royal manor house is believed to have existed on this site since the time of David I. Fire razed the manor in 1424, after which James I began construction of the present palace, a process that continued through two centuries and the reign of no fewer than eight monarchs. From the top of the northwest tower, Queen Margaret looked out in vain for the return of James IV from the field of Flodden in 1513. The ornate octagonal **fountain** in the inner courtyard, with its wonderfully intricate figures and medallion heads, flowed with wine for the wedding of James V and Mary of Guise. The last reigning monarch to stay in the palace was Charles I in 1633, though Bonnie Prince Charlie did stay for a night in 1745. The following year, in their haste to head north in pursuit of remaining Jacobites, the Duke of Cumberland's troops left the palace on fire, and it has been in ruins ever since.

This is a great place to take children: the rooflessness of the castle creates unexpected vistas and the elegant rooms with their intriguing spiral staircases seem labyrinthine. The galleried **Great Hall** is magnificent, as is the adjoining kitchen, which has a truly cavernous fireplace. Don't miss the dank downstairs **brewery**, which produced vast quantities of ale; 24 gallons was apparently a good nightly consumption in the sixteenth century.

Linlithgow is twenty minutes by rail from Waverley and there are trains throughout the day, approximately every half-hour.

STIRLING CASTLE

Map 1, A4. Daily: April–Sept 9.30am–6pm; Oct–March 9.30am–5pm; £4.

Stirling Castle must have presented would-be invaders with a formidable challenge. Its impregnability is most daunting when you approach the town from the west, from where the sheer, 250-foot drop down the side of the crag is most obvious. The rock was first fortified during the Iron Age, though what you see now dates largely from the fifteenth and sixteenth centuries. Presently undergoing a massive restoration scheme (due to be completed in 2001), small parts of the castle may be inaccessible.

The **visitor centre** (same times as castle) on the esplanade shows an introductory film giving a potted history of the castle, but the best place to get an impression of its gradual expansion is in the courtyard known as the **Upper Square**. Here you can see the magnificent **Great Hall** (1501–3); with its lofty dimensions and huge fireplaces, it is perhaps the finest medieval secular building in Scotland. The exterior of the **Palace** (1540–2) is richly decorated with grotesque carved figures and Renaissance sculpture, including, in the left-hand corner, the glaring bearded figure of James V in the dress of a commoner. Inside in the royal apartments are the **Stirling Heads**, 56 elegantly carved oak medallions, which once comprised the ceiling of the Presence Chamber, where visitors were presented to royalty. Otherwise the royal apartments are bare, their emptiness emphasizing the fine dimensions and wonderful views. The **Chapel Royal** (1594) was built by James VI for the baptism of his son, and replaced an earlier chapel, not deemed sufficiently impressive. The interior is lovely, with a seventeenth-century fresco of elaborate scrolls and patterns.

The castle also houses the impressive Argyll and Sutherland Highlanders **museum**, with its collection of well-polished silver and memorabilia, including a seemingly endless display of Victoria Crosses won by the regiment. The setup in the recently restored castle **kitchens** re-creates the preparations for the spectacular Renaissance banquet given by Mary, Queen of Scots for the baptism of the future James VI. As well as an audiovisual display describing how delicacies for the feast were procured, and an abundance of stuffed animals in various stages of preparation (who, we are assured, died natural deaths), the kitchens feature *faux* recipe books with such delights as sugar wine-glasses, golden steamed custard and dressed peacock.

From the **Douglas Gardens** you can see the surprisingly small window from which the eighth Earl of Douglas, suspected of treachery, was thrown by James II in 1452. There is a bird's-eye view down to the **King's Knot**, a series of grassed octagonal mounds which in the seventeenth century were planted with box trees and ornamental hedges.

STIRLING CASTLE

Stirling is 45 minutes by train from Waverley Station and trains depart approximately every half-hour. The castle is around a ten-minute walk from Stirling Station.

DIRLETON CASTLE

Map 1, G4. April–Sept Mon–Sat 9.30am–6.30pm, Sun 2–6pm; Oct–March Mon–Sat 9.30am–4pm, Sun 2–4pm; £2.

Dirleton Castle, located in the delightful village of Dirleton about fifteen miles east of Edinburgh, is largely in ruins, but the wonderful walled gardens are well worth the expedition.

As you pass through the gatehouse, look upwards to the "murder hole", a circular opening in the roof, once used for dropping objects onto the heads of unwelcome visitors.

Inside, turn left to see the **Lord's Hall**, a large room with a beautiful domed ceiling. This is part of the original castle built in the early thirteenth century by the de Vaux family, who also owned the island of Fidra in the Firth of Forth, visible to the north from the battlements of the castle. Over the next two hundred years, the Halyburtons built the eastern front, notable for the massive **Great Hall**. The most recent part of the castle is the **Ruthven Lodging**, a Renaissance house north of the original tower, built for the Ruthven family, whose propensity for skulduggery, including the murder of **David Rizzio** and the kidnapping of **James IV**, eventually led to the confiscation of the castle in 1600. Fifty years later, Dirleton, like the nearby Tantallon Castle, was bombarded by Cromwell's troops and destroyed.

The **gardens**, however, have thrived and still receive much attention. Apart from the sixteenth-century bowling green and the herbaceous border, look out for the belvedere just inside the entrance and a 400-year-old dovecote in the northeastern corner of the grounds.

TANTALLON CASTLE

Map 1, G4. April–Sept Mon–Sat 9.30am–6.30pm, Sun 2–6.30pm;
Oct–March Mon–Wed & Sat 9.30am–4.30pm, Thurs 9.30am–noon,
Sun 2–4.30pm; £1.50.

Around five miles east of Dirleton, next to the A198, is
Tantallon Castle. An enormous red sandstone ruin,
Tantallon is defended on three sides by sheer drops to the
sea and on the fourth by a double moat. While the English
ambassador, Sir Ralph Sadler, stayed in Tantallon for a time
in 1543, he wrote to Henry VIII: "Tantallon is of such
strength as I need not to fear the malice of mine enemies."

Built at the end of the fourteenth century, the castle was a
stronghold of the Douglases. Tantallon was besieged several
times before it was finally destroyed by Cromwell in 1651
after a twelve-day bombardment. The ruins, including a seventeenth-century dovecote left untouched by Cromwell's
men, have a wonderfully photogenic setting, with the Bass
Rock and the Firth of Forth in the background. You can
also walk along the cliffs from North Berwick.

CRICHTON CASTLE

Map 1, G6. April–Sept Mon–Sat 9.30am–6.30pm, Sun 2–6.30pm;
£1.50.

Although located close to what was once the principal
route south from Edinburgh, **Crichton Castle** is hidden
away on a hillock in a valley almost untouched by the
twentieth century.

Originally owned by the local Crichton family, the castle
passed into the hands of the **Earls of Bothwell** at the end
of the fifteenth century. Its earliest surviving feature, a rec-
tangular tower house, dates from the late fourteenth century and lies to the right of the entrance, while the startling

diamond-shaped facade on the courtyard wall was part of a new lodging added in the late sixteenth century by the flamboyant fifth Earl of Bothwell. He broke further with tradition by installing Scotland's first non-spiral staircase in the northern corner of the arcade. Described by a contemporary as "a terror to the most desperate duellists of Europe", Bothwell fled Scotland in 1595 and the king ordered the destruction of the castle. Thankfully, it was allowed instead to decline, in the words of Sir Walter Scott, into "remains of rude magnificence".

Crichton Castle is about eight miles south of Edinburgh. Take the A68 through Dalkeith; at the start of the village of Pathhead, turn right down the B6367 for about two miles and park next to the fifteenth-century Crichton Church, also built for the powerful Crichton family, from where the castle is a five-minute walk across a field.

ROSSLYN CHAPEL

Map 1, E6. April–Oct Mon–Sat 10am–5pm, Sun noon–4.45pm; Nov–March Mon–Sat 10am–5pm, Sun noon–4pm; £2.25. Bus #87A from the city centre.

The tranquil village of Roslin lies seven miles south of the centre of Edinburgh. An otherwise nondescript place, the village does boast the richly decorated late Gothic **Rosslyn Chapel**. Only the choir, Lady Chapel and part of the transepts were built of what was intended to be a huge collegiate church dedicated to St Matthew: construction halted soon after the founder's death in 1484, and the vestry built onto the facade nearly 400 years later is the sole subsequent addition. After a long period of neglect, a massive restoration project has recently been undertaken: a canopy has been placed over the chapel which will remain in place for several years in order to dry out the saturated ceiling and

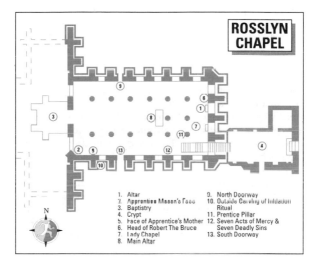

1. Altar
2. Apprentice Mason's Face
3. Baptistry
4. Crypt
5. Face of Apprentice's Mother
6. Head of Robert The Bruce
7. Lady Chapel
8. Main Altar
9. North Doorway
10. Outside Carving of Initiation Ritual
11. Prentice Pillar
12. Seven Acts of Mercy & Seven Deadly Sins
13. South Doorway

walls, and other essential repairs are due to be carried out within the chapel.

The outside of the chapel bristles with pinnacles, gargoyles, flying buttresses and canopies, while inside the foliage carving is particularly outstanding, with botanically accurate depictions of over a dozen different leaves and plants. Among them are cacti and Indian corn, providing fairly convincing evidence that the founder's grandfather, the daring sea adventurer Prince Henry of Orkney, did indeed, as legend has it, set foot in the New World a century before Columbus. The rich and subtle figurative sculptures have given Rosslyn the nickname of "a Bible in stone", though they're more allegorical than literal, with portrayals of the Dance of Death, the Seven Acts of Mercy and the Seven Deadly Sins.

ROSSLYN CHAPEL

The greatest and most original carving of all is the extraordinary knotted **Prentice Pillar** at the southeastern corner of the Lady Chapel. According to local legend, the pillar was made by an apprentice during the absence of the master mason, who killed him in a fit of jealousy on seeing the finished work. A tiny head of a man with a slashed forehead, set at the apex of the ceiling at the far northwestern corner of the building, is popularly supposed to represent the apprentice, his murderer the corresponding head at the opposite side. The entwined dragons at the foot are symbols of Satan, and were probably inspired by Norse mythology.

A number of books have been published in recent years about Rosslyn Chapel, drawing on everything from Freemasons and the Turin Shroud to the True Gospels and the regular sightings of UFOs over Midlothian. Conspiracy theories notwithstanding, the chapel is well worth a visit.

LISTINGS

9	Accommodation	97
10	Eating	111
11	Drinking	139
12	Live music and clubs	149
13	Theatre, comedy and cinema	156
14	Art galleries	161
15	Gay Edinburgh	164
16	Kids' Edinburgh	168
17	Shopping	172
18	Festivals and events	182
19	Directory	190

ACCOMMODATION

As you might expect from such a popular tourist destination, Edinburgh offers a more extensive choice of **accommodation** than anywhere else in Britain outside London. The majority of places to stay can be found in the streets immediately north of Haymarket Station, Royal Terrace and the lower reaches of the New Town, and to the south, around the inner suburbs of Bruntsfield and Newington, where numerous hotels and guest houses line the major roads into the city.

In addition to Edinburgh's **hotels**, hundreds of private houses provide **guest-house** accommodation. There's also a decent choice of both official and private **hostels**, and three **campsites** attached to caravan parks. Surprisingly though, the wide range of **campus accommodation** on offer is neither as cheap nor as convenient as might be expected.

The telephone code for Edinburgh is ☎0131.

Advance reservations are strongly recommended during the Festival: turning up without booking will mean accepting whatever is left (which is unlikely to be good value) or having to commute from the suburbs. The **tourist office**

sends out accommodation lists for free and can reserve any type of accommodation in advance for a non-refundable £3 fee: phone, call in personally when you arrive, or write in advance to Edinburgh Marketing Central Reservations Department (for details see p.5) stating requirements. In Waverley Station, Thomas Cook runs a hotel reservation service (daily 7am–10.30pm; ℐ556 0030) which makes a £5 non-refundable charge for bookings.

Accommodation price codes

In this section accommodation **prices** have been graded using the numbers below, according to the cost of the least expensive double room in high season. Bear in mind that many places raise their prices for the weekends of rugby internationals, for Christmas, for Hogmanay, and during the Festival.

① under £40	③ £50–60	⑤ £70–80	⑦ over £100
② £40–50	④ £60–70	⑥ £80–100	

HOTELS

Edinburgh's **hotels** are generally of a high standard and cover a wide range of tastes, from the hub of New Town elegance to quieter retreats out of the centre.

OLD TOWN

Apex International Hotel

Map 3, C4. 31–35 Grassmarket ℐ300 3456; fax 220 5345.
Formerly a student residence, this big, new, rather utilitarian hotel in the heart of the Old Town offers amazing views across to the castle from the upper floors and from the rooftop bar and restaurant. ④

HOTELS

Point Hotel

Map 3, A5. 34–59 Bread St ©221 9919; fax 221 9929.
Converted from a former Co-op, this large hotel is ideally
located for the Old Town and theatreland. Rooms are
comfortable and well-equipped, though the sombre colour
scheme and minimalist furnishings in the entrance hall take
some getting used to. Lively ground-floor restaurant, with two
course lunch for £7 and jazz on Saturdays. ⑥

NEW TOWN

Albany Hotel

Map 4, J2. 39–43 Albany St ©556 0397; fax 557 6633.
Three Georgian houses make up this hotel situated in a central
yet quiet location. High-ceilinged rooms have recently
undergone a complete revamp. *Haldane*'s restaurant in the
basement has quickly garnered favourable comments (see
p.118). ⑦

Balmoral Hotel

Map 4, K6. 1 Princes St ©556 2414; fax 557 3747.
Originally known as the *North British*, this Edinburgh landmark
has all the facilities of a top-class hotel, including a swimming
pool and gym. Its famous 192ft-high clock tower runs 2min
fast for the benefit of those hurrying to catch a train at
Waverley Station. ⑦

Caledonian Hotel

Map 4, D8. Princes St ©459 9988.
Like the *Balmoral*, this red sandstone building is a local
landmark. A luxury hotel at the west end of Princes Street
with fantastic views of the castle, providing every service you

HOTELS

could possibly desire. Also home to the *Pompadour*, a top-of-the-range formal French restaurant (see p.116). ⑦

Clifton Private Hotel

Map 2, A8. 1 Clifton Terrace ℂ & fax 337 1002.
Informal hotel opposite Haymarket Station. A reasonably priced choice for the area, with small but comfortable rooms and a pleasant south-facing lounge. ③

Greenside Hotel

Map 7, F3. 9 Royal Terrace ℂ & fax 557 0022.
Located on a quiet street with great views from the top floors across to Leith and beyond to the Firth of Forth. Fifteen rooms, all en suite, some suitable for families. Evening meals are available in the residents' bar; snacks can be rustled up at any time. Value for money considering the location. ⑤

Parliament House Hotel

Map 7, D4. 15 Calton Hill ℂ478 4000.
Smart new hotel in great central location halfway up Calton Hill; includes three rooms for disabled visitors. Converted from a town house and former council offices where Irvine Welsh used to work (and apparently where he wrote *Trainspotting*). No restaurant but numerous options in the vicinity. ⑥

Roxburghe Hotel

Map 4, B7. 38 Charlotte Square ℂ225 3921; fax 220 2518.
Another Edinburgh landmark, this upmarket traditional hotel contains antique furniture fireplaces designed by Adam and stands on the corner of his greatest creation, Charlotte Square. ⑦

Camore Hotel

Map 1, E4. 7 Links Gardens ✆ & fax 554 7897.

Georgian house overlooking Leith Links and up to Calton Hill and Arthur's Seat. Many attractive original features including marble fireplaces and ten rooms, four of which are en suite. Small bar and evening meals. ⑤

Malmaison Hotel

Map 1, E4. 1 Tower Place ✆555 6868; fax 555 6994.

In spite of its unlikely setting near Leith docks this is a great hotel with exceptionally helpful staff. Well away from busy roads so it's extremely quiet: a great place to watch dawn rise over the city docks and the Firth of Forth. ⑥

Allison House Hotel

Map 2, H9.15–17 Mayfield Gardens ✆667 8049; fax 667 5001.

Twenty-four rooms in this busy family-run southside hotel. Bar and restaurant offering "Taste of Scotland" menu for £16.75 also open to non-residents. Free car parking. ③

Arthur's View Hotel

Map 2, H9. 10 Mayfield Gardens ✆667 3468; fax 662 4232.

Pleasant hotel in convenient southside location. Twelve en-suite rooms. Bar meals with the accent on traditional Scottish fare. ⑤

Prestonfield House Hotel

Map 2, H9. Priestfield Rd ✆668 3346; fax 668 3976.

This luxurious hotel used to comprise just five rooms in a seventeenth-century mansion: a harmonious new wing has

HOTELS

increased this to 31, but it still feels intimate. The old house is full of unexpected delights, including two splendid lounges – the Leather Room and the Tapestry Room – while outside you can see peacocks strut on the lawns. ⑦

GUEST HOUSES

Although the price of staying at one of Edinburgh's many **guest houses** is rising steadily, they are relatively good value for money and generally have much more atmosphere than the larger city hotels. Many are large, elegant Georgian or Victorian houses, and can be found not only in the wide streets of the **New Town**, where there is a large and varied choice, but also slightly further from the middle of town on the major routes into Edinburgh, notably in the south of the city round **Newington** and the north of the city along **Ferry Road**.

NEW TOWN

Ardenlee Guest House

Map 2, E2. 9 Eyre Place ☏556 2838.
There are plants everywhere in this large guest house near the Botanic Gardens. The decor is restrained but attractive in the large family rooms, and the dining room has a display of old and new maps of Edinburgh. Vegetarian options on offer for breakfast. Private parking. Non-smoking. ③

Balmoral Guest House

Map 1, E4. 32 Pilrig St ☏554 1857.
Just five rooms, all immaculate and comfortable, in this cosy guest house. Great breakfast room with a Welsh dresser and

other more quirky pieces of furniture. Good family en-suite room and unrestricted parking. ①

Dickie Guest House

Map 2, F2. 22 East Claremont St ©556 4032.
Refreshingly unchintzy B&B not far from the centre of town. Tasty Scottish breakfasts. Very well-run and the owners are friendly and helpful. ③

Drummond House

Map 4, H1. 17 Drummond Place © & fax 557 9189.
Located on a quiet square in the centre of the New Town, this is the place for anyone seeking luxury without the pomp of a big hotel. Only four rooms available, so booking is advised. TV in the lounge only. Great breakfasts. Non-smoking. ⑥

No. 1 Bed and Breakfast

Map 2, H3. 1 Gayfield Place ©557 4752.
This pleasant B&B on the fourth floor of an Edinburgh tenement has just four rooms, all comfortable with small attic-style windows. The lounge has stunning views across to Calton Hill. There's a lot of choices for breakfast, and vegans are also catered for. Great for anyone who wants to be in the middle of the city. Book in advance. ②

Seventeen Abercromby Place

Map 4, G3. 17 Abercromby Place ©557 8036; fax 558 3453.
Fantastic New Town house once the home of William Playfair, one of Edinburgh's greatest architects. Its atmosphere is more that of a private home than a guest house; the decor throughout is lavish but stops short of being totally over-the-top. Some bedrooms are in converted stables. Private parking. Non-smoking. ⑦

GUEST HOUSES

Sibbet House

Map 4, F2. 26 Northumberland St ✆556 1078; fax 557 9495.
A special place in the heart of the New Town, this compact guest house is very much a family affair. Beautifully decorated rooms, and great personal attention from the owners. The host has been known to play the bagpipes at breakfast. Non-smoking. ⑤

Six Mary's Place

Map 2, B3. 6 Mary's Place, Raeburn Place ✆332 8965; fax 534 7375.
Very popular Stockbridge guest house renowned for excellent vegetarian breakfasts served in the bright conservatory (evening meals are also available). In summer, you can relax at night in the garden. A wonderful place. Non-smoking. ⑥

LEITH AND INVERLEITH

Brig O'Doon Guest House

Map 1, E4. 262 Ferry Rd ✆552 3953; fax 551 4797.
One of several good-quality guest houses on this stretch of road, affording wonderful views all the way from the Pentland Hills across to Arthur's Seat. Seven rooms, including five en suite. Unrestricted parking. ②

Park View Villa Guest House

Map 1, E4. 254 Ferry Rd ✆552 3456.
Unusually spacious guest house with six en-suite rooms, two of which are suitable for families. Tasty vegetarian options available for breakfast, plus a great lounge with fantastic views of the city. ②

SOUTH OF THE CENTRE

Hopetoun Guest House

Map 2, H9. 37 Mayfield Rd ℗667 7691.

Bright guest house with just three rooms which share two bathrooms. Great views of Arthur's Seat and Blackford Hill and plenty of buses into the centre. Non-smoking. ⑤

Kenvie Guest House

Map 2, H9. 16 Kilmaurs Rd ℗ & fax 668 1964.

Comfortable, homely guest house in quiet residential street close to the Royal Commonwealth Pool. Lots of buses into town. Full of interesting plants, with a wide choice of food for breakfast, plus tea and coffee. Some non-smoking rooms. ②

Ravensneuk Guest House

Map 2, H9. 11 Blacket Ave ℗ & fax 667 5347.

Built in 1836 in an exclusive conservation area, this family-run guest house is close to Holyrood Park and the city centre. Seven rooms, three of which are en suite. Fresh fruit salad and yoghurt available for breakfast. Non-smoking. ③

Rowan Guest House

Map 2, H9. 13 Glenorchy Terrace ℗ & fax 667 2463.

Victorian guest house located in a quiet residential street, yet close to bus routes into the middle of town. Nine rooms, including three en suite. Porridge and home-made scones for breakfast. ②

Turret Guest House

Map 2, H9. 8 Kilmaurs Terrace ℗667 6704; fax 668 1368.

Fascinating Victorian building with all sorts of detail, arches

GUEST HOUSES

and stairs, and a host of unusual gewgaws. Six rooms, two of which are reserved for smokers, and one four-poster bed. Order your breakfast the night before from a big menu: brave souls can try haggis or clootie dumpling (a traditional fruit cake from Dundee). ⑤

EAST OF THE CENTRE

Devon House Guest House

Map 1, F4. 2 Pittville St ✆ & fax 669 6067.
On a quiet side street, with pleasant parks and great walks along the promenade nearby. Good breakfast menu. ②

Joppa Turrets Guest House

Map 1, F4. 1 Lower Joppa ✆669 5806.
On the promenade at Portobello, this well-appointed guest house has fantastic views across the Firth of Forth and there's a sandy beach just a few yards away. ①

Stra'ven Guest House

Map 1, F4. 3 North Brunstane Rd ✆669 5580; fax 657 2517.
Very close to the beach, with seven rooms and a large, magnificent lounge. Very relaxed atmosphere. Unrestricted parking. Non-smoking. ②

CAMPUS ACCOMMODATION

With a large number of students studying in Scotland's capital, **campus accommodation** is available at certain times of the year: what's on offer varies from tiny single rooms in long lonely corridors to relatively comfortable places in small shared apartments. However, most of the colleges are not only a long way from the middle of town, but also quite costly.

Pollock Halls is the most central of the three options given here; **Jewel**, **Esk** and **Napier** are in the east and south of the city respectively. The three places we've reviewed below are open during Easter and for much of the summer.

Jewel and Esk Valley College

Map 1, F4. 24 East Milton Rd ℡657 7523.
Well-equipped rooms plus a small swimming pool. Roughly five miles east of the centre, close to the end of the A1. Bus #44 takes you into the middle of town. ②

Napier University

Map 2, C9. Craiglockhart Campus 219 Colinton Rd ℡455 4921.
In the southwest of the city. Buses #23 and #27 will take you to Princes Street; minimum stay two nights. ⑥

University of Edinburgh Pollock Halls of Residence

Map 6, A3. 18 Holyrood Park Rd ℡667 1971.
Beautifully located next to Arthur's Seat and the Royal Commonwealth Pool. ③

HOSTELS

If you're travelling on a budget, Edinburgh is fortunate in having several excellent **hostels**, including some located in the heart of the Old Town. At most of these you can expect to pay around £10 a night. The hostels listed below cover private establishments and those affiliated to the Scottish Youth Hostel Association (SYHA), both usually offer bunk-bed accommodation in single-sex dormitories and some have double rooms.

HOSTELS

Belford Hostel

Map 2, A7. 6–8 Douglas Gardens ℡225 6209.
Converted Victorian church west of the city centre, close to St Mary's Cathedral and the Gallery of Modern Art. Facilities include a laundrette, licensed bar, cable TV, lounge and pool table. Good self-catering facilities; breakfast also available. Dorm beds (4–8 per room) and doubles. No curfew. Open all year.

Bruntsfield Hostel

Map 2, C9. 7 Bruntsfield Crescent ℡447 2994.
SYHA youth hostel, on Bruntsfield Links in the south of the city, around a mile from Princes Street; take bus #11, #15 or #16. 2am curfew. Closed Jan.

College Wynd Youth Hostel

Map 3, G3. 205 Cowgate ℡226 2353.
Self-contained apartments suitable for groups of four to five people. Advance bookings through Edinburgh District Office ℡229 8660. Open June–Aug only.

Cowgate Tourist Hostel

Map 3, G3. 112 Cowgate ℡226 2153.
Another Cowgate summer-only hostel. Clean rooms in small apartments with private kitchens. Ideal location for exploring the Old Town nightlife. Laundry facilities available. No curfew. Open July–Sept.

Edinburgh Backpackers Hostel

Map 3, F8. 65 Cockburn St ℡539 8695.
Big hostel with a great central location in a side street off the Royal Mile. Very close to bus and rail stations. Self-catering kitchen, cable TV, storage, games room. A few doubles, mostly

dormitory accommodation. No curfew, so you can sample the nearby nightlife till the early hours. Open all year.

High Street Hostel

Map 3, F8. 8 Blackfriars St ☏557 3984.
Large, busy hostel just off the Royal Mile. Self-catering facilities if you wish, but breakfast is also available. Good atmosphere. Open 24hr, all year.

Iolare Guest House

Map 1, E4. 14 Argyle Place ☏667 9991.
In fact this is more a hostel than a guest house, offering basic accommodation with beds in dorms or twins for around £10 per person. Pleasant conservatory at the back of the house. Good cooking facilities and cheap fruit and veg shops over the road. Just across the Meadows, a short walk from the middle of town. Laundry facilities. No curfew. Open all year.

Royal Mile Backpackers

Map 3, E8. 105 High St ☏557 6120.
This hostel is about as central as you can get. Ambience will be familiar to all long-term travellers – busy dormitories, with lots of people lolling about. Open all year.

CAMPSITES

There are three well-equipped campsites within the Edinburgh city boundaries: one in the west and two in the north of the city. Although each is a fair distance from the middle of town, all are well served by buses. You can expect to pay under £10 a night for a tent.

CAMPSITES

Mortonhall Caravan Park

Map 1, B6. 38 Mortonhall Gate, East Frogston Rd ©664 1533.
Five miles from the centre in the south of the city near the
Braid Hills; take bus #11 from Princes Street. Laundry
facilities. Around 250 places, play area and three toilet/shower
blocks. Open March–Oct.

Silverknowes Caravan Site

Map 1, C4. Marine Drive, Silverknowes ©312 6874.
Very busy campsite in the west of the city. Not a great part of
town, but you don't have to spend much time here as it's just a
half-hour bus (#14) journey from the middle of town. Close to
sea and Lauriston Castle. Room for 100 tents. Open
April–Sept.

Slatebairns Caravan Club Site

Map 1, E6. Roslin, Midlothian ©440 2192.
This is an attractive countryside site with good facilities for
caravans and tents, and is only seven miles from the city centre
(bus #87A). Open Easter–Oct.

EATING

You can eat well in Edinburgh on almost any budget, and choose from pretty much any international cuisine. Plenty of places specialize in **traditional Scottish cooking**, using fresh local produce, while the city's ethnic communities, despite their small size, have drastically improved the **restaurant** scene, with some great **Italian** trattorias and a host of excellent **Indian** restaurants serving regional dishes. In addition, the application of home-grown ingredients to classic Gallic recipes is something the city does particularly well, resulting in some fabulous **French** restaurants. **Vegetarians** and vegans are well catered for, and there are plenty of **fish** specialists — seafood fans should head to **Leith**, whose waterside restaurants serve consistently good food. Most of Edinburgh's restaurants serve from noon to 2.30pm and 6pm to 11pm and close on Sundays, except where otherwise stated in our reviews. During the Festival, however, the majority of restaurants stay open all day until the early hours. Bear in mind that Edinburgh has a fairly high turnover of restaurants — some of impeccable repute have bitten the dust in the past few years — and don't be surprised if one or two listed here have closed by the time you read this.

Remember also that distinctions between cafés and restaurants are sometimes blurred, as many of the newer establishments, though called cafés, are restaurants (or at least brasseries) in all but name. Our list sections essentially run through the best places to eat, beginning with cafés and brasseries – if what you want is a quick, unpretentious bite to eat, or even just a coffee – followed by types of cuisine subdivided alphabetically.

The city has nothing approaching the **café** society of other European capitals, but if you fancy a snack there are a growing number of good establishments serving cakes and sandwiches. When choosing a place to eat, bear in mind that most **pubs** serve food, and that many have a restaurant attached.

....

If you'd prefer to make your own meals, see p.178
for details of the best places to buy food.

....

The large city-centre hotels also have restaurants, but most of these are extremely expensive. In the listings below, **prices** are indicated as inexpensive (under £10); moderate (£10–20); expensive (£20–30) and very expensive (over £30), excluding the cost of **drink**. Most places have a ten percent service charge. The majority of places reviewed below accept all major types of **credit cards**; we've indicated those which don't.

OLD TOWN

BRASSERIES AND CAFÉS

Blue

Map 3, A4. 10 Cambridge St ℂ221 1222.
Daily: noon–3pm & 6pm–midnight. Moderate.
Bright new minimalist café on the first floor of the Traverse Theatre (see p.159). Relaxed atmosphere; pop in any time for a coffee and tasty snack or have a reasonably priced full meal. Desserts are totally scrumptious and bread is divine.

City Café

Map 3, G4. 19 Blair St ☏220 0125.
Daily: 11am–11pm. Inexpensive.

This trendy café with slightly faded Fifties chic serves cheap soup, baked potatoes and sandwiches for lunch and fills up with bright young things in the evening.

Clarinda's

Map 3, I8. 69 Canongate ☏657 1888.
Mon–Sat 8.30am–4.45pm, Sun 10am–4.45pm. Inexpensive.

Located near the foot of the Royal Mile, this snug café serves breakfasts, excellent home baking and light lunches. Its traditional service is a bit old-fashioned, but it's friendly and you get locals popping in for a chat.

Common Grounds

Map 3, E2. 2–3 North Bank St ☏226 1146.
Mon–Fri 9am–11pm, Sat & Sun 10am–11pm. Inexpensive.

American-style coffee shop on two levels. Menu includes filled croissants, quiches and a good range of wonderfully flavoured coffees. Anyone struggling to get through the day should try the "Keith Richards". Live music most evenings. Non-smoking upstairs.

Deacon's Café

Map 3, D8. 3 Brodie's Close, 304 Lawnmarket ☏226 1894.
Daily: 9am–early evening, later during the Festival. Inexpensive.

This is the place to go if you just want a light snack while you're out sightseeing. Look for the figure of Deacon Brodie beckoning you down a Royal Mile close and relax with sandwiches, scones and coffee, or something a bit stronger on a cold day.

BRASSERIES AND CAFÉS: OLD TOWN

Elephant House

Map 3, E4. 21 George IV Bridge ℗225 6267.
Mon–Sat 7.30am–10pm, Sun noon–8pm. Inexpensive.

Elephants and Sloaney-type students of every shape and size surround you in this highly popular café which offers a large selection of coffees and teas with croissants and pastries. Great views of the castle from the back room and a selection of board games for those with time to kill. Claims to be designed according to *Feng Shui* principles.

Elephant's Sufficiency

Map 3, E8. 170 High St ℗220 0666.
Daily winter 8am–5pm, during the Festival 8am–midnight. Inexpensive.

Good drinks and a decent range of modest snacks, soup, burgers, filled rolls and pastries – all you could want from this unpretentious café on the Royal Mile. Also does takeaway.

Iguana

Map 3, F5. 41 Lothian St ℗220 4288.
Daily: 9am–1am. Moderate.

Nineties-style twisted metal stairs and vivid orange walls make this a trendy hangout for pre-club crowd. All-day food includes a sizeable vegetarian breakfast, couscous, roasted aubergines and pan-fried chicken with lime. The TVs show videos made by local artists.

Lower Aisle

Map 3, E8. High Kirk of St Giles, High St ℗225 5147.
Mon–Fri 9.30am–4.30pm. Inexpensive.

Located in the crypt of St Giles, you can smell the baking as you look round the church. This is the place to go for home-made quiches, baked potatoes and salads or to mingle with lawyers from the neighbouring courts. Does the trick both for a mid-morning drink and for a light lunch.

Patisserie Florentin

Map 3, D8. 8–10 St Giles St ⓒ225 6267.
Mon–Fri 7am–midnight, Sat & Sun 7am–2am. Inexpensive.
French-style café on two floors, just off the High St. Exquisite pastries and delicious coffee downstairs. Some hot food served upstairs. Trendy late-night hangout; office crowd during the day.

FRENCH

L'Auberge

Map 3, G9. 58 St Mary's St ⓒ556 5888.
Mon–Sat 12.15–2pm & 6–10pm, Sun 12.15–2pm & 6–9.15pm. Very expensive.
Great French restaurant using top Scottish ingredients, smoked salmon, and the best cuts of meat. Huge wine list with wines from all over France. Intimate atmosphere, attentive service.

Grain Store

Map 3, E3. 30 Victoria St ⓒ225 7635.
Mon–Fri noon–3pm & 5.30–11pm, Sat noon–4pm & 5.30–11pm, Sun noon–10pm. Moderate.
Another reasonably priced, solid Scottish/French restaurant in a large alcoved first-floor room. Starters include salads and seafood; for main course try guinea fowl and venison or a vegetarian special. Great cheeseboard from Iain Mellis's wonderful shop below (see p.180). £12.50 for a two-course dinner.

FRENCH: OLD TOWN

Pierre Victoire

Map 3, E3. 10 Victoria St ☎225 1721.
Daily: noon–4.30pm & 5pm–1am. Moderate.

The immensely successful chain of cheap French restaurants started in Edinburgh by Pierre Levicky still offers good value, especially at lunch, when the flagship three-course lunch is just £4.90, with dishes such as sautéed chicken or beef casserole. Dinner is more expensive at £10.90. Cosy and friendly atmosphere.

Pompadour

Map 3, A3. Caledonian Hotel, Princes St ☎459 9988.
Tues–Sat 7.15–10.15pm. Very expensive.

The *Pompadour*, which takes its name from Madame De Pompadour, the mistress of Louis XV, is the place for a very special occasion. If the sumptuous setting – all draped curtains, murals and over-the-top plasterwork – doesn't do it for you, then the top-quality French cuisine will. Jacket and tie required for men.

Le Sept

Map 3, E8. Old Fishmarket Close ☎225 5428.
Mon–Thurs noon–2.15pm & 6–10.30pm, Fri noon–11.30pm, Sat noon–10.30pm, Sun 12.30–2.15pm & 6–10pm. Moderate.

Down an attractive High Street Close near the Fringe Office. Three-course set lunch for £6.50, three course set dinner for £12. Excellent fish and steak and a wide selection of crêpes for vegetarians. On fine days you can sit outside.

INDIAN

Spices

Map 3, D4. 110 West Bow ☎225 5028.
Mon–Fri noon–2pm, Sat 6–11pm. Moderate.

Slightly unusual design with pictures of Indian movie stars on the plain walls, this offshoot of the *Kalpna* (see p.133) presents a small but reliable menu. Apart from chicken and lamb dishes, you can have aubergines with hot chillies or a tasty vegetable navratan. Set lunch for £5.95, more for dinner.

ITALIAN

Beppe Vittorio

Map 3, E3. 7 Victoria St ⌀226 7267.
Mon–Sat noon–3pm & 5.30–11pm, Sun noon–4pm & 6–10pm. Moderate.
This pleasant restaurant offering simple, moderately priced Italian food is part of the ever-expanding *Pierre Victoire* empire. Great veal, seafood and fish and a somewhat unusual display of nightwear strung across a washing line at the rear of the restaurant

Mamma's

Map 3, C4. 30 Grassmarket ⌀225 0404.
Sun–Thurs noon–10.30pm, Fri & Sat noon–11pm Inexpensive.
Ever fancied haggis pizza? You can choose your own dream combination from 49 toppings (at the last count) at this lively American-style pizzeria. Tables outside in the summer and reasonably priced wine. Basically a good fun place to eat

---

For reviews of the best child-friendly cafés and restaurants, see p.170.

SCOTTISH

The Atrium

Map 3, A4 10 Cambridge St ⌀220 8882.
Mon–Fri noon–2.30pm, Sat 6–10.30pm. Expensive.
Often described as Edinburgh's best restaurant, this tastefully decorated room inside the Traverse Theatre has hand-crafted

ITALIAN & SCOTTISH: OLD TOWN

lighting and railway sleeper tables and offers imaginatively cooked food using top-quality ingredients. At lunchtime you can have tempting snacks, such as chicken liver parfait or a risotto for around £5, or a full meal for £20. An evening meal, with a range of delights like baked halibut with honeyed aubergine, will cost you rather more. Great wine list.

Creelers

Map 3, F8. 3 Hunter Square ✆220 4447.
Mon–Thurs noon–2.30pm & 5.30–10.30pm, Fri & Sat noon–2.30pm & 5.30–11pm. Moderate.
Attractive, bright seafood restaurant, with paintings on show, priding itself on using the freshest Scottish produce and serving oysters, langoustines, scallops or mussels for starters, turbot, monkfish and hake for the main course. Lunch £7.50, supper £16.50. Some tables outside in the summer.

Jacksons

Map 3, E8. 209 High St ✆225 1793.
Daily: noon–2pm & 6–10pm. Inexpensive.
Classy basement restaurant in an old town close, using the best Scottish produce, such as venison, Aberdeen Angus beef, wild boar and salmon. Two course set lunches cost £4.95; table d'hôte dinners from £21.95. Finish off with a malt whisky from a choice of over fifty brands. Very popular with tourists.

SPANISH

El Bar

Map 3, G9. 15 Blackfriars St ✆558 9139.
Daily: noon–1am. No cards. Inexpensive.
Atmospheric tapas bar with sandwiches and a range of

delicious Spanish nibbles: tortillas, chorizo, cheese and ham.
A few Mexican favourites as well, accompanied by lively
Spanish music to get you in the mood. Quiet by day, hectic at
night.

Igg's

Map 3, G2. 15 Jeffrey St ℗557 8184.
Mon–Sat noon–2.30pm & 6–10.30pm. Expensive/Very expensive.
A Spanish-owned hybrid, offering tapas snacks and
Mediterranean dishes, plus traditional Scottish food. Not great
for veggies but plenty of tasty fish. Good lunchtime tapas from
around £5. Early evening three course meals are £18.50; after
7.30pm an à la carte meal will cost you about £30.

VEGETARIAN

Bann's Vegetarian Café

Map 3, F8. 5 Hunter Square ℗226 1122.
Daily: 10am–11pm. Inexpensive.
Varied selection of vegetarian food, with a standard menu
of veggie burgers, curries, enchiladas, organic beer and
wine and a blackboard list of daily specials. You can eat well
for under £10. Some tables outside for the summer
months.

Black Bo's

Map 3, G9. 57–61 Blackfriars St ℗557 6136.
Mon–Sat noon–2pm & 6–10.30pm, Sun 6–10.30pm. Moderate.
Renowned for unlikely but successful combinations, such as
deep-fried mint and tofu balls or haggis and garlic cream
cheese strudels. Two courses at lunchtime for £5.50. The
atmosphere here is relaxed, though there's a lively bar next
door.

SPANISH & VEGETARIAN: OLD TOWN

NEW TOWN

Catwalk Café

Map 2, G3. 2 Picardy Place ✆478 7770.
Daily: 9am–1am. Moderate.

The latest and highly successful attempt to open a bar in a
prime New Town setting has created a smart street-side café
upstairs, and a cool hangout downstairs with unadorned white
walls and minimalist furniture. Unfinished look throughout
with concrete stair slabs and unisex sinks outside the toilets.
This café, dishing up excellent breakfasts and Mediterranean-
style lunches during the day, is transformed after 6pm into a
busy pre-club venue.

Cyberia

Map 4, G6. 88 Hanover St ✆220 4403.
Mon–Sat 11am–10pm, Sun noon–7pm. Inexpensive.

At times there's a tangible buzz in this light and airy Internet
café which offers a decent range of teas, coffees, croissants and
sandwiches. Half an hour surfing the Net costs from £2.50.
The café is licensed, has art exhibitions and offers training
courses for using the nine machines.

Laigh Bake House

Map 4, G6. 117a Hanover St ✆225 1552.
Mon–Sat 8.30am–4pm. Inexpensive.

Long-established, homely New Town cafe with flagstone floor
and cast-iron stoves. Good salads and soups, but best known for
its wonderful home-baked scones and cakes.

Patisserie Florentin

Map 4, C2. 5 North West Circus Place ©220 0225.
Daily: 7am–7pm. Inexpensive.
Compact branch of the Old Town patisserie, this one has a
mouthwatering shop with a dazzling display of bread and
pastries. Some tables outside in the summer.

Terrace Café

Map 2, C1. Royal Botanic Garden ©552 0616.
Daily: March–Oct 10am–5pm; Nov–Feb10am–2.30pm. Inexpensive.
Fantastic location offering stunning views of the length of the
Royal Mile. Reasonable food but not ground-breaking
Sandwiches, baked potatoes and cakes, juices for younger visitors.

Valvona and Crolla

Map 2, H2. 19 Elm Row ©556 6066.
Mon–Sat 8am–5pm. Inexpensive.
Winner of best newcomer restaurant in 1996, Edinburgh's
finest deli now has a café at the back of the shop. Filled
focaccias, exotic salads and some hot dishes. Select any wine
from the front shop: £2 corkage.

AMERICAN

Smoke Stack

Map 4, L1. 53–55 Broughton St ©556 6032.
Daily: noon–10.30pm. Moderate
You won't go hungry in this stylish American restaurant with
minimalist furnishings and wooden floors. Huge portions of
chargrilled meats; two course lunch for £6.50 and Scottish
snails and frog's legs for starters. Sunday brunch will cost you
about £7.

AMERICAN: NEW TOWN

CHINESE

Bamboo Garden

Map 4, E5. 57a Frederick St ✆225 2382.

Mon–Fri noon–2pm & 5–11pm, Sat & Sun noon–midnight. Moderate.

Basement restaurant with a big selection of banquets and a meal for seven for £17.50 a head. Full meals or weekend dim sum sessions can all be catered for here. Vegetarian dishes on offer, but ring in advance for full veggie banquets.

Kweilin

Map 4, F1. 19 Dundas St ✆557 1875.

Tues–Thurs noon–10.45pm, Fri & Sat noon–11.45pm, Sun 5–10.45pm. Moderate.

Long-running busy Cantonese restaurant that passes the acid test of popularity with the local Chinese community. Large menu with lots of seafood. Three course dinner for £16.50.

Loon Fung

Map 2, 1D. 2 Warriston Place ✆556 1781.

Mon–Fri noon–midnight, Sat 2pm–1am, Sun 2pm–midnight. Moderate.

Excellent Cantonese restaurant offering a big spread of dim sum dishes, with plenty of seafood and vegetarian options. Other dishes to go for include squid in black bean sauce, and crispy seaweed.

FRENCH

Café St Honoré

Map 4, G4. 34 Thistle St Lane ✆226 2211.

Mon–Fri noon–3pm & 7–10pm, Sat 7–10pm. Moderate.

On a city-centre side street, this popular New Town restaurant has been done up to look like a Parisian brasserie. Serving

French cooking with fashionable influences from points further east. Tasty bread, and scrumptious puddings. Non-smoking.

La Cuisine d'Odile

Map 2, B5. French Institute, 13 Randolph Crescent ©225 5685.
Tues–Sat noon–2pm, closed Sun & Mon. No cards. Inexpensive.
Lunchtimes only for this highly regarded French restaurant in the West End. Sublime French home cooking at £6.50 for three courses.

Maison Hector

Map 2, B3. 47 Deanhaugh St ©332 5328.
Sun–Thurs 11am–midnight, Fri & Sat 10.30am–1am.
Moderate/Expensive.
Trendy Stockbridge postmodernist café. Luxurious seating in the bar at the front, a more private restaurant to the rear, with the kitchen visible through a screen. Baguettes and snacks at lunchtime, French/Scottish cuisine at night. Wheelchair access.

FISH AND SEAFOOD

Café Royal Oyster Bar

Map 4, K5. 17a West Register St ©556 4124.
Mon–Sat noon–2pm & 7–10.15pm, Sun 12.30–2.30pm & 7–10.15pm. Very expensive.
Now known by everyone as the restaurant featured in *Chariots of Fire*, you can't miss the classy stained-glass windows showing various sporting activities. Oysters from the west of Scotland, and all sorts of fish dishes. Alternatively turn up on Sunday for a sumptuous brunch, starting from £12.50, which includes blueberry muffins and a glass of buck's fizz. Somewhere you'll remember.

FISH AND SEAFOOD: NEW TOWN

Indian Cavalry Club

Map 2, A7. 3 Atholl Place ☎228 3282.
Daily: noon–2.30pm & 5.30–midnight. Moderate.
Upmarket West End establishment serving rich flavours but nothing too hot. Good wine list at reasonable prices. A two course lunch costs £6.95 and five course evening banquet will set you back £15.95.

Lancers

Map 2, C3. 5 Hamilton Place ☎332 3444.
Daily: noon–2.30pm & 5.30–11.30pm. Moderate/Expensive.
Upmarket Stockbridge restaurant, offering Bengali and North Indian cuisine. For a real gourmand experience, the Kurji lamb, a whole leg of lamb marinated in herbs and barbecued, costs £69.95 for four people. Three course lunchtime thalis cost £7.95 (vegetarian) and £9.95 (meat).

ITALIAN

The Patio Restaurant

Map 4, G5. 87 Hanover St ☎226 3653.
Mon–Sat 11.30am–2pm & 5–11pm. Moderate.
Friendly family-run establishment with great seafood and a big range of pasta dishes. Popular venue for office nights out and family occasions.

Tinelli

Map 2, K2. 139 Easter Rd ☎652 1932.
Mon–Sat noon–2.30pm & 6–10.30pm. Moderate.
Worth a detour to an otherwise unlikely part of town for this very popular restaurant, often said to be Edinburgh's best

Italian. Small but interesting menu, no background music, attentive service. Interesting combinations of food, including pumpkin-filled pasta.

Vito's

Map 4, E5. 55a Frederick St ©225 5052.
Daily: noon–2.30pm & 6–11pm. Moderate/Expensive.
Bustling basement restaurant providing quality Italian cooking at mid-range prices. A three course lunch costs £8.50. The à la carte menu has an excellent range of seafood dishes, such as pan-fried prawns on mushrooms.

MEXICAN

Blue Parrot Cantina

Map 2, C3. 49 St Stephen's St ©225 2941.
Mon–Thurs 5–11pm, Fri & Sat noon–11pm, Sun 5–10.30pm. Moderate.
Cosy Stockbridge basement restaurant, with a small, frequently changing menu. For starters you can have one of the Mexican staples, nachos and guacamole, while main courses include delights such as haddock in lime and coriander sauce. Two courses at lunchtime for £5.

MOROCCAN

The Marrakech

Map 2, F3. 30 London St ©556 7293.
Mon–Sat 6.15–10pm. Moderate.
The owners are from Rabat, rather than Marrakesh, but this is a great little restaurant, housed in the basement of a small hotel. The fare offers Moroccan staples, delicately spiced *tajines* (meat or fish stews), couscous and wholesome *harira* (chickpea broth). There's a wonderful home-cooked bread, too, and Moroccan pastries. Unlicensed but no corkage if you bring your own bottle.

MEXICAN & MOROCCAN: NEW TOWN

Duck's at Le Marché Noir

Map 2, E2. 2–4 Eyre Place ✆558 1608.
Mon–Fri noon–2.30pm & 7–10.30pm, Sat & Sun 6.30–9.30pm.
Expensive/Very expensive.
Scottish cuisine with a considerable French influence, most
notably manifest in a huge wine list and some seriously
expensive cognacs. Three course dinner for £26. Regional
evenings with a five course meal for £38 on last Sunday of the
month. One non-smoking room.

Haldane's

Map 4, J2. 39 Albany St ✆556 8407.
Mon–Fri noon–2pm & 6.30–9.30pm, Sat 7–10.30pm. Expensive.
An elegant restaurant located in the basement of the *Albany
Hotel* that looks like the dining room of a country hotel.
Lunch offers relatively informal possibilities like soups and
sandwiches, while dinner gives you the chance to sample some
beautifully presented dishes made with the very best Scottish
ingredients.

Martin's

Map 4, C7. 70 Rose St, North Lane ✆225 3106.
Tues–Fri noon–2pm, Sat 7–10pm; closed Sun & Mon. Very
expensive.
Don't be put off by the lacklustre surroundings: this
luxurious restaurant has a great reputation locally. Game and
seafood from the west coast of Scotland feature prominently
amongst the main courses on a small menu which has a
wealth of wild and organic produce on offer. Renowned
cheeseboard.

SCOTTISH: NEW TOWN

36

Map 4, E1. 36 Great King St ℃556 3636.
Mon–Sat noon–2.30pm & 6–10.30pm, Sun noon–2pm & 7–9.30pm.
Very expensive.

Very chic minimalist restaurant in the basement of the decidedly upmarket *Howard Hotel*. The decor may be minimal but the top-quality Scottish food is given lavish attention. Start off with smoked salmon, then try scallops or goose breast before finishing off with yummy home-made ice cream.

SOUTHEAST ASIAN

Buntoms

Map 4, H1. 9 13 Noloon St ℃557 4044.
Mon 6–11pm, Tues–Sat noon–2pm & 6–11pm, Sun 7–11pm. Moderate.

Edinburgh's longest-running Thai restaurant in part of a New Town hotel has now been going for ten years. Three course lunch for £6.50, evening banquet is £19 (minimum four people). Don't miss the tom yum soup with prawns.

The Kris Restaurant

Map 2, I3. 20a Leopold Place ℃557 1225.
Mon–Sat noon 2pm & 5–10.30pm. Moderate.

Basement restaurant just around the corner from the Playhouse serving all the usual; coconut, chilli and lemon grass dishes. Tuesday sees a vegetarian buffet for £12.50, while the full Malaysian buffet on Wednesday costs £15.50.

Siam Erewan

Map 4, E3. 48 Howe St ℃226 3675.
Mon–Sat noon–2.30pm & 6–11pm, Sun 6–11pm. Moderate

Quality Thai restaurant with good use of exotic and fresh fruit and vegetables. Steamed prawns, crispy Thai pancakes and

SOUTHEAST ASIAN: NEW TOWN

curries of varying degrees of heat. Three course lunch for
£6.95, evening banquets up to £19.95.

Singapura

Map 4, D5. 69 North Castle St ✆538 7878.
Mon–Thurs noon–2.30pm & 6–10.30pm; Fri noon–2.30pm &
6–11.30pm, Sat 12.30–2.30pm & 6–11.30pm, Sun 6–10.30pm.
Moderate.

Smart New Town location for a restaurant playing up colonial
connections with Singapore with a display of old photographs,
pith helmets and trunks. The food shows influences from all
over East Asia, with hot Thai curries, spicy Chinese tofu and a
delicious Indonesian gado-gado salad. Wash it down with
Tiger Beer from Singapore or choose from a decent selection
of European wines.

Tampopo

Map 4, F5. 25a Thistle St ✆220 5254.
Daily: noon–2.30pm & 6–10pm. No cards. Inexpensive.

Small Japanese noodle shop, with a name familiar to film
buffs. Very plain decor, this is a fast-food establishment with
filling bowls of noodle soup for around £5; flavours include
vegetable and seafood. Not licensed. Also does takeaway.

SPANISH

The Tapas Tree

Map 2, H2. 1 Forth St ✆556 7118.
Daily: 11am–11pm. Moderate.

Good fun, extremely authentic tapas bar dishing up all those
holiday favourites – patatas bravas, squid in batter, aubergines –
accompanied by Spanish classical guitar on Monday and
Wednesday evenings.

SOUTHEAST ASIAN & SPANISH: NEW TOWN

Henderson's Salad Table

Map 4, G4. 94 Hanover St ☎225 2131.
Mon–Sat 8am–10.45pm. Inexpensive.

Edinburgh's first vegetarian restaurant has been going for
thirty years and is still just about the best. Large selection of
hot dishes, backed up with a dozen or so salads. Leave room
for the great puddings or something off the oozing
cheeseboard. It's self-service, however, so don't be surprised to
find a long queue.

LEITH

Malmaison Café Bar

Map 1, E4. 1 Tower Place ☎555 6969.
Daily: noon–2.30pm & 6–10.30pm. Expensive.

French-style brasserie with a pleasant atmosphere. Small menu
covers steak frites, chargrilled chicken and salmon fishcakes
and sumptuously rich potato purée. Alternatively you could
try the adjacent vegetarian café for a selection of salads and
sandwiches.

Sirius Bar

Map 1, E4. 10 Dock Place ☎555 3344.
Mon–Wed & Sun 11.30am–1am, Thurs–Sat 11.30am–2am. Moderate.

Seriously cool 1990s bar named after a locally built ship in the
heart of Leith. All muted colours and low tables. Pasta and
salads for lunch, Thai stir-fries or chicken couscous for
something more substantial.

Yee Kiang

Map 1, E4. 42 Dalmeny St ©554 5833.
Tues–Sun 5.30–11.30pm. Moderate.

Small homely restaurant off Leith Walk where the most
popular dishes are chicken and cashew nuts in a yellow bean
sauce and aromatic crispy duck. Peking duck, which will set
you back £25, must be ordered in advance. A few vegetarian
options. Peking dinner for two for £19.

FISH AND SEAFOOD

Marinette

Map 1, E4. 52 Coburg St ©555 0922.
Tues–Sat noon–2pm & 6–10pm. Expensive.

The light-coloured walls and fishnets provide a Mediterranean
ambience, enhanced by the wonderful food. For starters, try the
bouillabaisse; for a splurge go for the £24 seafood platter.
Otherwise try a sauce such as meunière, ginger and coriander
or thyme and lemon to go with the fish of the day. A few meat
options.

The Shore

Map 1, E4. 3–4 The Shore ©553 5080.
Mon–Sat noon–2.30pm & 6.30–10.30pm, Sun 12.30–3pm &
6.30–10pm. Moderate.

Best bet here is to go for the fresh fish, monkfish, halibut or
sea bass, cooked in a variety of styles. Good veggie options
and tasty pistachio ice cream. All in a delightful non-smoking
dining room with a view over the harbour. For an informal
meal, you can also eat in the bar accompanied by jazz or folk
music.

Skipper's

Map 1, E4. 1a Dock Place ℰ554 1018.
Mon–Sat 12.30–2pm & 7–10pm. Expensive.

One of the quieter and more discreet of the Leith restaurants; good for a romantic meal. Best not to stray too far from the wonderful selection of fish dishes. Three course dinners cost £19.75.

The Vintner's Rooms

Map 1, E4. The Vaults, 87 Giles St ℰ554 6767.
Mon–Sat noon–2.30pm & 7–10.30pm. Very expensive.

Luxurious restaurant in a former wine warehouse off a cobbled courtyard. Top-class imaginative cooking with intriguing ingredients and combinations such as guinea fowl with lentils. Crème brûlée features among the puddings and there's a huge wine list with bottles starting from around £10. This is *the* place for a special occasion.

Waterfront Wine Bar

Map 1, E4. 1c Dock Place ℰ554 7427.
Mon–Thurs noon–2.30pm & 6.30–9.30pm, Fri & Sat noon–3pm & 6–10pm, Sun 12.30–3pm & 6–9pm. Moderate.

One of the earliest of the current boom in Leith restaurants and still very busy in spite of all the competition. As elsewhere in the locality, the accent is on fresh fish. The lengthy wine list has a good reputation. Go for the three course lunch at £7.

INDIAN

The Raj Restaurant

Map 1, E4. 89–91a Henderson St ℰ553 6968.
Mon–Thurs & Sun 5.30–11.30pm, Fri & Sat 5.30pm–midnight. Moderate.

Quality cooking from Goa and Bangladesh in a large bright restaurant that was once a cinema with a great view over the

INDIAN: LEITH

water of Leith. Cheap prices from Sunday to Thursday, when 1983 prices are on offer. Lunches are £4.95 during the week and £6.95 at weekends. Various culinary accoutrements also on sale.

ITALIAN

Silvio's

Map 1, E4. 54 The Shore ℃553 3557.
Mon–Sat noon–2pm & 6–10.30pm. Inexpensive.

A variety of fresh pastas and delicious grilled antipasti, both meat and vegetable. Meat and fish dishes for main course. Charming, attentive staff and a pleasant riverside setting. Two course lunch for £10.50. Non-smoking.

SCOTTISH

(Fitz)henry

Map 1, E4. 19 Shore Place ℃555 6625.
Mon–Thurs 12.30–2.30pm & 6.30–10pm, Fri & Sat 12.30–2.30pm & 6.30–10.30pm, closed Sun. Expensive/very expensive.

Spacious brasserie in a Leith backstreet housed in a converted seventeenth-century warehouse, with flagstone floors and plastered walls. Mostly French with a few additional flavours thrown in. Three course dinner for £22, two course lunch from £10.

THE SOUTHSIDE

BRASSERIES AND CAFÉS

Metropole

Map 2, H9. 33 Newington Rd ℃668 4999.
Daily: 10am–10pm. Moderate.

Relaxed Art Deco café in a former bank where you can have

just a piece of quiche and a coffee while you read a newspaper.
Soups, sandwiches and cakes also on offer. Handy place for
anyone staying out in Newington. Non-smoking.

Maxie's Bistro and Wine Bar

Map 2, H8. 32b West Nicolson St ℗667 0845.
Mon–Thurs 11am–midnight, Fri & Sat 11am–1am. Moderate.
Basement bistro handily placed for quick pre-show meals.
Good-quality French-style seafood, meat and veggie dishes
washed down with an excellent selection of wine and decent
beer. At lunchtime you can have two courses for £3.95, while
the evening menu offers three courses for £9.95.

Nicolson's

Map 2, H8. 6a Nicolson St ℗557 4567.
Daily: 9am–midnight. Inexpensive.
Spacious first-floor café opposite the Festival Theatre.
Mediterranean cuisine with many vegetarian options. Two course
lunches for £7.50.

CHINESE

Chinese Home Cooking

Map 2, H9. 34 West Preston St ℗668 4946.
Sun–Thurs 5.30–11pm, Fri & Sat 5.30–11.30pm. Inexpensive.
This cheap-and-cheerful Chinese restaurant is very popular
with students. Try the three course lunch at £4, or the three
course dinner for £6. Specialities include steamed fish.

FRENCH

La Bonne Vie

Map 2, H9. 49 Causewayside ℗667 1110.
Daily: noon–2.30pm & 6–10.30pm. Moderate.
Excellent intimate French restaurant specializing in game

CHINESE & FRENCH: THE SOUTHSIDE

and fish. Starters range from duck liver parfait to marinated melon topped with bacon, while for main course you can have the likes of chargrilled salmon or venison and beef casserole. Three courses for £6.95 at lunch, £14.95 at night.

INDIAN

Kalpna

Map 2, H9. 2 St Patrick Square ①667 9890.
Mon–Sat noon–2pm & 5.30–11pm; closed Sun, except during Festival. Moderate.

Long-standing vegetarian restaurant offering southern Indian food. At lunchtime, eat as much as you wish for £4.50; evening menus and thalis are around £10. Functional decor but beautifully cooked food.

Khushi's Lothian Restaurant

Map 2, H7. 16 Drummond St ①556 8996.
Mon–Thurs noon–3pm & 5–9pm, Fri & Sat noon–3pm & 5–9.30pm. No cards. Inexpensive.

Distinctly unpretentious Indian café that has been an Edinburgh institution for forty years. A small menu of Punjabi dishes including plenty of vegetarian options. You can bring in a pint of lager from *Stewart's* bar next door.

Suruchi

Map 2, H8. 14a Nicolson St ①556-6583.
Daily noon–2pm & 5.30–11.30pm. Moderate.

Excellent Indian restaurant for a quick meal either before or after a show at the Festival Theatre directly opposite: mostly vegetarian, with some chicken dishes. Regular Food

Festivals emphasizing regions of India. Jazz nights on Wednesdays and Fridays. Three course lunch £4.95, dinners £9.95.

MEXICAN

Mother's

Map 2, I9. 107-9 St Leonard's St ℗667 0772.
Mon–Thurs 6–10pm, Sat & Sun 6–10.30pm. Moderate.
All the usual Mexican favourites, with enchiladas and chimichanga well to the fore. Plenty of alternatives, including pasta and steaks, and pies galore for pudding – from Mississippi mud to pecan. Happy hour 6–7pm.

NORTH AFRICAN

Phenecia

Map 2, H8. 55 West Nicolson St ℗662 4493.
Mon–Sat noon–2pm & 6–11pm, Sun 6–10pm
Inexpensive/Moderate.
Eclectic cheap restaurant, serving north African and Mediterranean dishes. Delicious hummus and couscous. Three course lunches cost under £5.

SCOTTISH

Kelly's

Map 2, H8. 46b West Richmond St ℗668 3847.
Wed–Sat noon–2pm & 7–9.30pm; closed Sun–Tues. Expensive.
This long-standing restaurant has recently changed hands but maintains previous high standards, serving modern British cooking in a calm, intimate setting using the best and freshest ingredients. Changing menus, with the possibility of lobster or

MEXICAN, NORTH AFRICAN & SCOTTISH: THE SOUTHSIDE

barbary duckling, will not disappoint those with a taste for the exotic. Dinner £25.

VEGETARIAN

Engine Shed

Map 2, I9. 19 St Leonard's Lane ℰ662 0042.
Daily: Lunchtimes only. Mon–Thurs 10.30am–3.30pm, Fri 10.30am–2.30pm, Sat 10.30am–4pm, Sun 11am–4pm. No cards. Inexpensive.

Worth taking a detour to this excellent vegetarian restaurant near Pollock Halls. Soups, salads, veggie stews and baked potatoes, and there's a wonderful bakery on the premises.

LOTHIAN ROAD AND TOLLCROSS

BRASSERIES AND CAFÉS

Cornerstone Café

Map 2, C6. St John's Church, Princes St ℰ229 0212.
Mon–Sat 9.30am–4.30pm. Inexpensive.

Self-service café in the undercroft of St John's Church at the corner of Princes Street and Lothian Road. Mostly veggie and very reasonably priced, with soup from £1 and hot dishes from £2.50. A few tables outside during summer.

Ndebele

Map 2, C9. 57 Home St ℰ221 1141.
Daily: 10am–10pm. Inexpensive.

Named after a southern African tribe, this bright, vibrant café is a welcome newcomer. For around £2.50 have a sandwich and salad (the mustardy salad dressing is great); otherwise try something more exotic like Boerwass, a spicy South African sausage. All washed down with fruit juice or African coffees and teas. Also does takeaway and sells African knick-knacks.

Jasmine

Map 2, C7. 32 Grindlay St ℗229 5757.
Mon–Thurs noon–2pm & 5–11.30pm, Fri 5pm–12.30am, Sat 2pm–12.30am, Sun 2–11.30pm. Moderate.
The long-standing *Loon Fung* has a new name and management but the menu has been left almost untouched. Cantonese cooking with a strong seafood bias: choose from oysters with ginger and spring onion, deep fried squid, or the succulent crispy monkfish in a honey sauce. Also some meat and veggie dishes. Lunch is £6.50.

Lee On

Map 2, C9. 3–4 Bruntsfield Place ℗229 7732.
Mon–Thurs noon–2pm & 5.30pm–midnight, Fri & Sat noon–2pm & 5.30pm–1am, Sun 5.30pm–midnight. Moderate.
Restaurant just up from the *King's Theatre* with simple decor and quality Cantonese cooking. Excellent hot and sour soup and seafood dishes. Three course lunches for £3.80.

La Bagatelle

Map 2, D9. 22a Brougham Place, Tollcross ℗229 0869.
Mon–Sat noon–2pm & 6–10.30pm, Sun 6–10pm. Moderate/Expensive.
French cuisine of a very high standard. Hot smoked salmon among the starters and rich sauces for the meat or fish main courses. Lunch is £8.50 for three courses.

Shamiana

Map 2, D9. 14 Brougham Place, Tollcross ℂ229 5578.
Mon–Sat 6–10pm, Sun 6–9pm. Moderate.

Award-winning north Indian and Kashmiri restaurant located in a tasteful environment midway between the *Kings* and the *Lyceum* theatres. Successful enough to open in the evening only. Worth booking in advance.

Stac Polly

Map 2, C7. 8a Grindlay St ℂ229 5405.
Map 4, J2. New Town 29–33 Dublin St ℂ556 2231.
Mon–Fri noon–2pm & 6–11pm, Sat 6–11pm. Expensive.

Tastefully decorated, calm restaurant. Game, fowl and fish, with good Scottish ingredients. Scottish beef, turbot and monkfish or, for the adventurous, wild duck with rhubarb and almond crumble. Two course set lunch for £9.95. Special pre- and post-theatre dinners for around £14.

DRINKING

D rinking is one of Edinburgh's real pleasures. Many of the city's **pubs**, especially in the Old Town, are hundreds of years old, while others, particularly in the New Town, are unaltered Victorian or Edwardian period pieces that rank among Edinburgh's most outstanding examples of interior design. Add in the plentiful supply of trendy modern bars, and there's a variety of styles and atmospheres to cater for all tastes. Many honest *howffs* or drinking dens stay open late and, during the Festival especially, it's easy to find bars open until at least midnight.

Most of the city's pubs now sell "real ale", cask-conditioned beer in various strengths made by Scottish breweries like the giant Scottish and Newcastle, who produce McEwan's and Younger's ales. The small independent Caledonian Brewery uses old techniques and equipment to produce some of the best beers in Britain, and there's also the tiny Rose Street Brewery, which has its own pub.

During the summer the Caledonian Brewery, Slateford Road (©337 1286) runs tours for groups of twenty or more; phone ahead to arrange a visit.

Edinburgh's main drinking strip is the near-legendary **Rose Street**, an unremarkable pedestrianized lane tucked between Princes and George streets in the New Town; the ultimate Edinburgh pub crawl comprises drinking a half-pint in each of its dozen or so establishments – plus the two in West Register Street, its eastern continuation. Most of the pubs frequented by students are in and around **Grassmarket**, with a further batch on the **Southside**, an area overlooked by most tourists. **Leith** has a nicely varied crop of bars, ranging from the roughest spit-and-sawdust places to polished pseudo-Victoriana, while two of the city's best and most interesting pubs are further west along the seafront in **Newhaven**.

Pub and brewery tours

A nice way to structure your evening's drinking is to take the **Original Edinburgh Literary Pub Tour** (Thurs–Sun 6pm & 8.30pm; ©554 0777; £6), a well-presented tour of Scottish literary history around the renowned watering holes of the major figures of Scottish literature from Burns and Scott to McDiarmid and Welsh. Led by professional actors, the tour commences at the *Beehive Inn*, 18–20 Grassmarket, and a minimum of six people is needed for it to proceed.

OLD TOWN

Bannermans

Map 3, H3. 212 Cowgate.
Popular Cowgate cellar pub full of louche studenty types, drinking good real ales like Theakston's and Caledonian's. Cheap and filling lunches during the week. Formerly a vintner's cellar, with a labyrinthine interior. Exceptionally busy during Festival time. Best pub on the street.

Bar Kohl

Map 3, D9. 54 George IV Bridge.

Seriously cool bar, offering more than 250 varieties of vodka along with yummy sandwiches served up in New York style – thickly packed with adornments of your choice.

Black Bo's

Map 3, H3. 57–61 Blackfriars St.

Trendy Old Town bar, next to a veggie restaurant of the same name. Loud and funky music in the evenings, when things can get pretty wild.

Bow Bar

Map 3, D4. 80 West Row.

This old wood-panelled bar recently won an award as the best drinkers' pub in Britain, with a connoisseur's selection of over a hundred malt whiskies and first-rate real ales, from north and south of the border; try Deuchar's or Orkney Dark Island if you get the chance. There are a few pies and rolls available, but drinking's the main business here.

Canon's Gait

Map 3, H8. 232 Canongate ©556 4481.

Cosy Royal Mile basement bar, with books and plates on the walls, so it's just as well things don't get too lively. The beer's good and there's a friendly unpretentious atmosphere. A mixture of folk and jazz nights.

Doric Tavern

Map 3, E2. 15 Market St.

A bar with an excellent brasserie which is well patronized by the beautiful people and journalists from the nearby

DRINKING: OLD TOWN

141

Scotsman. Great views over Princes Street. Downstairs, in stark contrast, is *McGuffie's Tavern,* a serious late-night drinking spot.

Fiddlers Arms

Map 3, C4. 9–11 Grassmarket.

Unspoiled city-centre pub serving McEwan's 80 shilling. The walls are adorned with forlorn, stringless violins, but others that are still intact are used for the live fiddling sessions which take place on Monday nights.

Green Tree

Map 3, H3. 184 Cowgate.

Patronized by students during term time and by just about everyone on warm August evenings, when the small walled garden is "standing room only" and there's limited room for drinking inside.

Jolly Judge

Map 3, D8. 7a James Court.

Romantically located down a close looking onto a large courtyard. One of the best of the touristy bars near the castle and it serves decent and reasonably priced lunchtime food.

Malt Shovel

Map 3, F2. 11–15 Cockburn St.

Just around the corner from the station, the *Malt Shovel* is a busy city-centre pub with a few cosy nooks for anyone seeking a bit of privacy. A choice of half a dozen ales and a hundred malt whiskies to go with great pub food.

Sandy Bell's

Map 3, E6. 25 Forrest Rd.
Revered Edinburgh institution with folk music sessions most
nights. Anyone in search of a quieter time could try the chess
night on Sunday or dominoes on Tuesday.

NEW TOWN

Abbotsford

Map 3, B1. 3 Rose St.
This upscale pub with original Victorian decor is one of the
finest in the city. Once the haunt of music-hall artists, now the
best place to start a crawl of the many Rose Street pubs. Good
food and ale, and a choice of over fifty malts. Closed Sundays.

Baillie Bar

Map 2, C3. 2 St Stephen St.
Busy basement bar at the corner of Edinburgh's most self-
consciously Bohemian street. Attracts a mostly young crowd,
along with the odd old-timer. Sandwiches and pub nosh served
at lunchtime and throughout the afternoon.

The Basement

Map 4, L1. 10a Broughton St.
Packed out, especially at the weekends, with a pre-club crowd,
this trendy bar is efficiently run by young and enthusiastic staff.
Mexican food served at the weekend, a two course set lunch
will set you back about £5.

Bert's Bar

Map 2, B3. 29 William St & 2–4 Raeburn Place.
A two bar chain, the one on William Street fills up with a

DRINKING: NEW TOWN

143

lunchtime office crowd, while the Raeburn Place branch is more of an evening hangout for Stockbridge yuppies. Both have excellent beer and good food. Well run by young and eager staff.

Café Royal

Map 4, K5. 17 West Register St.

Unmissable Edinburgh institution. The opulent late-Victorian *Circle Bar* on the ground floor has tiled portraits of famous inventors from William Caxton to James Watt. Sinks in the gents are hideously over-the-top.

Clark's Bar

Map 4, F1. 142 Dundas St.

Traditional no-nonsense Scottish bar at the foot of Dundas Street. Big rowdy bar in the front and more secluded rooms at the back. Very much a locals bar, though not at all unfriendly.

The Dome Bar and Grill

Map 4, C6. 14 George St.

No-expense-spared conversion of a bank patronized by local celebs. Several bars, the most dramatic being the former telling hall, decorated with a Greek cross and a huge central dome. The front bar is more sedate but no less opulent.

Guildford Arms

Map 4, K5. 1–5 West Register St.

A great city-centre Victorian bar, with an excellent selection of well-kept ales; look out for any of the Harvieston brews. Go up to the gallery to eat pub grub and observe the goings-on. Regular beer festivals.

DRINKING: NEW TOWN

Indigo Yard

Map 4, A7. 7 Charlotte Lane.

Very hip new West End bar built over a courtyard. Eastern influences feature prominently in the thirst-raising menu. There's a gallery bar for observing the bright young things.

Mathers

Map 4, L1. 25 Broughton St.

This traditional Edinburgh pub is the best place in Edinburgh for stout, with Guinness and Murphy's on tap, as well as the local Gillespie's. Always busy, frequented by staff from the nearby post office and a pre-club crowd.

Milne's Bar

Map 4, G4. 35 Hanover St.

Famous in the Fifties and Sixties as the meeting place of Hugh McDiarmid and other members of the Scottish literari. Check out the photos on the walls as you sample one of the ten real ales.

Oxford Bar

Map 4, C6. 8 Young St.

Unspoilt city-centre bar, popular with nearby office workers and rugby fans. A few snacks, but not enough to distract from the business of drinking.

Po-Na-Na

Map 4, E5. 43b Frederick St.

Is it a pub or a nightclub? Anyway, this trendy bar, will charge you to get in if you arrive after 11pm (Mon–Thurs & Sun £2, Fri & Sat £3) and you still might have to queue. DJs every night and some basic snacks. Open till 3am nightly.

Peartree House

Map 2, H8. 36 West Nicolson St.

The beer garden here, a rarity in the city centre, fills up quickly when the sun comes out. The self-service bar lunches are not bad; you pay by the size of the plate. Attracts students and the odd biker. Open until midnight.

Stewart's

Map 2, H7. 14 Drummond St.

A Southside institution since the beginning of the century, and looks like little has changed since then. Traditional no-frills Victorian drinking pub, with a large group of regulars augmented by students and passing iconoclasts.

Bennet's Bar

Map 2, C9. 8 Leven St, Tollcross.

The best of all Edinburgh's Victorian pubs, conveniently located near to cinemas and theatres. The front bar has decorative tiles and local maps under the glass-topped tables for working out where to go next, while the Green Room at the back and away from the TV is normally quieter. Good traditional pub lunches of steak pies and burgers.

Merman

Map 1, E4. 42 Bernard St.

Classic beer drinker's bar in the heart of Leith, with a great wee snug in the front and more space through the back. Always a good selection of real ales.

DRINKING: THE SOUTHSIDE & LEITH

Tattler

Map 1, E4. 23 Commercial St.
Bar-restaurant decked out in plush Victorian style and serving wonderful, award-winning meals of high-quality Scottish food including fish, meat and poultry.

NEWHAVEN

Starbank Inn

Map 1, E5. 64 Laverockbank Rd.
Fine old stone-built pub overlooking the Forth with a high reputation for cask ales and bar food.

Ye Olde Peacock Inn

Map 1, E5. Lindsay Rd, Newhaven.
Big and busy pub with all sorts of fish and chips on the menu. The Creel Lounge contains prints of the famous nineteenth-century photographs of Newhaven fishwives by Hill and Adamson.

SUBURBS

Athletic Arms (The Diggers)

Map 1, C4. 1 Angle Park Terrace West.
Out in the western suburbs, near Tynecastle football ground and Murrayfield rugby stadium, the pub's nickname comes from the cemetery nearby. For many years, *The Diggers* was a beer drinkers' oasis in a city full of keg beers. Other places have caught up but this is still worth a visit.

Caley Sample Room

Map 1, C4. 50 Angle Park Terrace West.
Large showpiece pub selling the range of cask ales produced by the Caledonian Brewery, just up the road. Also the place to try cask whiskies. Regular quiz nights.

Canny Man's (Volunteer Arms)

Map 2, C9. 237 Morningside Rd, Morningside.

Quirky pub in the heart of Morningside with all manner of weird and wonderful objects displayed. A pleasant beer garden for warm Morningside evenings.

Sheep Heid

Map 6, I6. 43 The Causeway, Duddingston.

Whether you've walked round Arthur's Seat or jumped on a bus to get to Duddingston, you shouldn't miss the opportunity to visit this sedate pub. Built in 1670, it's said to be the oldest licensed premises in Scotland. Beer garden and a skittle alley and good pub food, including a full roast dinner on Sundays.

Temple Hall Hotel

Map 1, E4. 77 Promenade, Portobello.

A seafront bar on Portobello Promenade with a beer garden for those rare balmy days. Decent beer and friendly staff.

LIVE MUSIC AND CLUBS

nevitably, Edinburgh's **nightlife** is at its best during the Festival (see p.183), which can make the other 49 weeks of the year seem like one long anticlimax. However, when not compared to this misleading yardstick, the city has a lot to offer, especially in the realm of **performing arts** and **live music**.

You can usually hear **jazz**, **folk** and **rock** every evening in one of the city's hundreds of pubs, but for the big rock events, other more versatile venues – such as the Castle Esplanade, Meadowbank Stadium and the exhibition halls of the Royal Highland Show at Ingliston, the site of occasional raves – are often pressed into service. Alternatively, Edinburgh has a number of venues for **classical music** and dance, including the Festival Theatre, which houses large-scale opera and ballet, and the Playhouse, where ballet is featured during the Festival. Usher Hall is the best place to find orchestral music, while smaller ensembles tend to perform at the Queens Hall. Choral and organ recitals are held at assorted venues, the best known being the High Kirk of St Giles. Check the press for details.

The **club scene**, while not offering anything startlingly original, comprises an array of alternating nights and changing fads, for example, Going Places, an immensely trendy easy listening night which is held every few weeks in a variety of venues. Elsewhere, a number of places have Seventies or Eighties nights with the emphasis firmly on fun, dressing up and drinking. In the bigger venues, you may find different clubs taking place on each floor. Most of the city-centre clubs stay open till around 3am.

The best way to find out **what's on** is to pick up a copy of *The List*, an excellent fortnightly listings magazine covering both Edinburgh and Glasgow (£1.90). Alternatively, get hold of the *Edinburgh Evening News*, which appears daily except Sunday: its listings column gives details of performances in the city that day, hotels and bars included. **Tickets** and **information** on all events are available from the tourist office (see p.5). Box offices of individual halls and theatres are likewise liberally supplied with promotional leaflets, and some are able to sell tickets for more than one venue.

LIVE MUSIC VENUES

Café Graffiti

Map 4, L2. Mansfield Place Church, at the foot of Broughton St ✆557 8003.

New club in the basement of a famous local church, where the hugely popular weekend nights get going around 10.30pm. It's worth arriving well before midnight, as the place sells out very quickly. Mostly large-scale Latin and jazz/soul bands.

Cas Rock Café

Map 3, B5. 04 W Port ✆229 4341.

Near the art college, a bastion of the Edinburgh pub-rock scene, the *Cas Rock* is used predominantly by local up-and–

coming bands and old-timers like the UK Subs. Also hosts an annual punk festival in the summer, when it fills up with Scandinavian and German mohicans.

The Queen's Hall

Map 2, H9. 37 Clerk St ℗668 3456.
Converted Southside church, with gigs from African, funk and rock bands on the way up or back down, as well as smaller jazz and folk concerts. The nearest to an intimate medium-sized music venue. Also hosts comedy nights with well-known comedians.

Royal Oak

Map 2, H7. 1 Infirmary St ℗557 2976.
Friendly, unpretentious folk bar. Music every night with local residencies and visiting artists in upstairs and downstairs bars. Feel free to join in and have a good sing-along.

Tap o'Lauriston

Map 3, D6. 80 Lauriston Place ℗229 4041.
Popular pub which attracts an alternative crowd from the nearby art school. You're unlikely to have heard of any of the bands that play here, though the names usually give the game away: unreconstructed punks and Goths. For a total contrast, the pub also has regular free evenings of local DJs playing techno.

Tron Ceilidh House

Map 3, F9. 9 Hunter Square ℗220 1500.
Cavernous pub, handily placed just off the High Street, with jazz and folk and a regular comedy spot on Friday nights. Can get very hot and busy.

LIVE MUSIC VENUES

The Venue

Map 7, B7. 15 Calton Rd ℗557 3073.
Indie bands, local and national, and the odd rock'n'roll legend.
Dark and dingy; just right for raucous guitar-based music.

CLASSICAL MUSIC

Reid Concert Hall

Map 2, G8. Bristo Square ℗650 4367.
Owned by Edinburgh University, this hall is used sparingly
during the year for classical music concerts. Free lunchtime
recitals of organ and piano music.

St Cecilia's Hall

Map 3, G3. Corner of Cowgate and Niddry St ℗650 2805.
The oldest purpose-built concert hall in Scotland, now owned
by Edinburgh University. The excellent collection of early
keyboard instruments is used during the Festival and
occasionally at other times. Acoustics are good but have to
compete with a noisy modern city right outside.

Usher Hall

Map 2, C7. Corner of Lothian Rd & Grindlay St ℗228 1155.
Large Edwardian concert hall, with a 2500 seating capacity.
Used for big-scale classical music events and by MOR pop and
country giants. Shortly to begin a long-overdue renovation
after a recent Tony Bennett concert almost brought the roof in.

NIGHTCLUBS

The Attic

Map 3, H3. Dyers Close Cowgate ℗225 8382.
In the heart of Edinburgh's clubland, this popular, medium-
sized venue can hold up to 300 people. Recently refurbished,

welcome new features include air-conditioning, new toilets and a spanking wooden floor. Try the Transporter Room on Wednesday nights for a hip mixture of live music and DJs.

La Belle Angèle

Map 3, G4. 11 Hasties Close ©225 2774.
Another revamped venue, Manga is a sizzling Friday night drum'n'bass club, other nights cover a broad spectrum from house and garage to Latin and hip-hop. Also used intermittently for live gigs, though this usually means that everything is all over by 10pm to make way for the later club night. Acts include indie and visiting African and Latin stars.

The Cavendish

Map 2, C9. 3 West Tollcross ©228 3252.
Sir Ossie's Mambo Club has been a weekend resident here for years, playing African and Latin sounds downstairs and reggae and dancehall upstairs. Weekday nights tend to be more studenty. Also used for live shows from Sixties and Seventies stalwarts, Mungo Jerry, Geno Washington, etc: on these occasions, it's over-25s only.

The Citrus

Map 2, C7. 40–42 Grindlay St ©622 7086.
Located in a former, rather soulless, student union, *The Citrus* is another venue to have received a recent face lift. Covers most mainstream styles from Eighties indie music to funk and disco. Popular reggae sounds on Sunday nights.

Club Mercado

Map 3, E2. 36–09 Market St ©226 4224.
Friday nights are popular with the after-office crowd who come for the Seventies Kerplunk night. Arrive early and dress

with style for Saturday nights, which alternate between house and glam. Also see the early evening (7.30-10.30pm) Snog for the under-18s.

Honeycomb

Map 3, G3. 36–38a Blair St ©220 4381.
Purpose-built venue opened in 1996, the *Honeycomb* has a superb sound system, with well-established Friday nights alternating between garage, hip-hop and house. Large enough to have two separate dance areas; at Saturdays' Groove Theory you can move between house in the main room and jazz-funk and disco classics in the back. The garage and house music presented at the Sunday night, Taste is rated by many to be Edinburgh's best night out. Alternatively you could try the live jazz sessions from Monday to Wednesday, including a Coltrane tribute every Tuesday night.

Jaffa Cake

Map 2, C7. 28 King Stables Rd ©229 7986.
Another former student union, so called for its three layers with orange in the middle. Normally a busy student nightclub, with the accent on indie and chart music. Staged the New Music Festival in August 1997, an attempt to bring popular music to the forefront of the Fringe Festival.

The Liquid Room

Map 3, D3. 9c Victoria St ©225 2564.
Large long-standing venue benefiting from an extensive refurbishment. Aiming for the student crowd with indie and chart nights and dance music. Big dance floor and a huge, powerful sound system.

NIGHTCLUBS

Negociants

Map 3, F5. 45–47 Lothian St ©225 6313.

The basement of a very popular bar close to the University, with different clubs every night of the week. Styles range through most forms of modern dance music, house, funk, soul and even some dub. Added attraction of decent beer. Free admission.

The Venue

Map 7, B7. 15 Calton Rd ©557 3073.

When it's not a seedy rock'n'roll pit, the *Venue* is a stomping nightclub with room for 1000, who can spread themselves out over three floors. A string of long-running nights is on offer, the best of which, both fortnightly, are Pure on Friday nights for techno and house, and the Saturday–night Tribal Funktion, which belts out house and garage soul. Other regular events cover a wide-ranging reggae extravaganza and a mixture of disco and funk nights. Attracts a very mixed crowd.

Wilkie House

Map 3, G3. Cowgate ©225 2935.

Excellent venue capable of taking up to 700 punters, and big enough to contain a handy chill-out room. Friday nights offer Sublime, a hectic trance night, while alternating Saturday nights include Joy, a long-running gay night and Vena, for progressive house.

THEATRE, COMEDY AND CINEMA

Edinburgh has a relatively small but thriving **theatre** and **cinema** scene. The Traverse leads the way for new live drama, the Royal Lyceum regularly stages top-quality work, often with a Scottish theme, while the **Festival Theatre** presents the biggest and most prestigious touring shows. The opening of the massive Festival Theatre in 1994 was a momentous occasion for a city which had for so long lacked a truly regal setting for grand opera. However, the new total of almost 11,000 seats in the capital which, outside Festival time, has a population of under half a million, has proved excessive, and in order to avoid competition the city council have joint management.

Ticket prices for live theatre vary enormously, ranging from £5 to £25 depending on the venue and the production.

> During the Festival, church halls, Masonic halls and
> even churches are used for the staging of dramatic
> performances. Check press for details.

Edinburgh has several multiscreen venues, and two excellent repertory **cinemas**, the Cameo and Filmhouse, both of which present a daily choice of arthouse and mainstream films. At the cinema you can expect to pay around £5 for an evening show; less during the day. Check with the venue or read *The List* or *The Scotsman* for details of performances and special offers for previews or reduced tickets for student card-holders.

THEATRE AND COMEDY

Assembly Rooms

Map 4, C6. 54 George St ℘220 4348.
Elegant eighteenth-century building used intermittently during the year for ceilidhs and music shows before becoming *the* Fringe venue, hosting everything from stand-up comedy to drama. Not the best place to watch a sensitive play, as you are likely to be disturbed by something more raucous taking place elsewhere in the building.

Bedlam Theatre

Map 3, E6. 2a Forrest Rd ℘225 9893.
A converted church which is another busy Fringe venue and for the rest of the year the main venue for productions by students from nearby Edinburgh University.

Church Hill Theatre

Map 2, C9. Morningoide Rd ℘220 4349.
A converted Victorian church which has been transformed into a rather utilitarian theatre, used mainly by local amateur dramatics groups and visiting festival groups.

THEATRE AND COMEDY

Festival Theatre

Map 2, H8. Nicolson St ℡529 6000.

Revamped music-hall theatre, now with a grandiose glass front, where fire claimed the life of a famous illusionist, the Great Lafayette, in 1911. Today, almost 2000 can enjoy an eclectic programme of theatre, music and, above all, opera in luxurious surroundings.

Gilded Balloon Theatre

Map 3, H3. 233 Cowgate ℡226 6550.

Year-round Friday-night comedy shows and wall-to-wall entertainment during the Festival. The Late'n'Live (1–4am) show is a Fringe institution, offering the chance to catch up on a wide range of well-known or emerging comedians.

King's Theatre

Map 2, H9. 2 Leven St ℡229 1201.

Long-running theatre offering a broad choice of popular visiting theatrical troupes. The most reliable place for TV star-led pantomime.

Netherbow Arts Centre

Map 3, E8. 43 High St ℡556 9579.

Compact venue offering a regular supply of up-to-date drama leavened with festivals of story-telling and puppetry. Has an attractive café.

Playhouse Theatre

Map 2, H3. 18–22 Greenside Place ℡557 2590.

Restored following a serious fire in 1993, the Playhouse is a huge theatre, seating around 3000, and is used most of the year for popular musicals and dance shows and for large-scale ballet shows at Festival time.

Pleasance Theatre

Map 2, H7. 60 The Pleasance ℭ556 6550.
Another busy Fringe venue staging comedy, theatre and the odd
bit of music. Some performances take place in the courtyard.

Royal Lyceum Theatre

Map 2, C7. 30 Grindlay St ℭ229 9697.
A very beautiful Victorian theatre with compact auditorium.
Busy year-round venue offering reliable mainstream drama.

St Bride's Centre

Map 2, A8. 10 Orwell Terrace ℭ346 1405.
Another converted church that doubles as a busy community
centre. Used by school groups and local dramatic societies
during the year and for a variety of shows at Festival time.

Traverse Theatre

Map 2, C7. 10 Cambridge St ℭ228 1404.
Edinburgh's premier venue for cutting-edge experimental
theatre, with regular offerings of new drama from Scottish and
international performers. Recent successes include a
production of David Greig's *Caledonia Dreaming*, about
Edinburgh folks' obsession with actor/superstar Sean Connery.

CINEMAS

Cameo

Map 2, C9. 38 Home St ℭ228 4141.
A three-screen venue with a plush main auditorium.
Specializes in arthouse, independent and cult movies, weekend
late-night shows for devotees of *Betty Blue* and *Reservoir Dogs*,
and interesting Sunday matinées. Also has a good bar.

Filmhouse

Map 3, A5. 88 Lothian Rd ©228 2688.

Eclectic programme of independent, art and classic films in a
converted church. Has recently installed new screens in the two
existing cinemas, as well as adding a new third screen. Main
centre for the Edinburgh International Film Festival. Excellent
bar/café with monthly film trivia quiz nights. Good facilities
for the disabled.

CINEMAS

ART GALLERIES

I n addition to the National Gallery (see p.60) and Gallery of Modern Art (see p.71) mentioned in earlier chapters, Edinburgh has a number of smaller specialist art galleries, where you can see both traditional Scottish painting, typified by landscapes of beautiful Highlands scenery, and more contemporary works by a new generation of successful young artists.

In general the ritzy upmarket venues, such as the **Scottish Gallery**, are in the New Town. The more modern and trendier spaces, like the **Collective Gallery**, can be found in the Old Town. Also in the Old Town are the **City Art Centre** and the **Fruitmarket Gallery**, where major exhibitions are mounted, and two dynamic photographic galleries, **Portfolio** and **Stills**. Many of the arts venues also have regular shows: there are exhibitions at Filmhouse, Queen's Hall and, particularly, Inverleith House in the Royal Botanic Garden. Check *The List* or *The Scotsman* for details of current shows.

City Art Centre

Map 4, I8. Market St ☏529 1033.
Mon–Sat 10am–6pm.
Big civic venue on four floors that is often used for blockbuster exhibitions: notable successes have included *Star Trek* and

Chinese Warriors. Choice items from the council's own substantial collection of art, including fascinating paintings of Edinburgh in former times, are also occasionally put on display.

Collective Gallery

Map 3, F2. 22–28 Cockburn St ℰ220 1260.
Tues–Sat 11am–5.30pm.
Now in its twelfth year, the Collective Gallery is run by a large group of artists and is an up-to-date space offering conventional and mixed-media shows. Recent efforts included a look at club culture. The Project Room, a small space off the main room, is used for smaller exhibitions.

Edinburgh College of Art

Map 3, D6. Lauriston Place ℰ221 6000.
Mon–Fri 10am–4pm, Sat 9am–1pm.
It's always worth checking out the degree show held here in the spring and there are regular exhibitions throughout the year, the most interesting often at the time of the Festival. Fabulous views of the castle from the upper floors.

Edinburgh Printmakers' Workshop

Map 2, G3. 23 Union St ℰ557 2479.
Tues–Sat 10am–6pm.
Used predominantly by local artists, but holding a special show for the Festival. Good place to go to buy reasonably priced screen prints and lithographs. Workshops and courses on offer.

Fruitmarket Gallery

Map 4, I8. Market St ℰ225 2383.
Tues–Sat 10.30am–5.30pm, Sun noon–5pm.
Popular large space presenting the best in contemporary art

ART GALLERIES

from Scotland and abroad in a variety of media. Regular exhibitions from high-profile international names.

Portfolio Gallery

Map 3, E4. 43 Candlemaker Row ⓒ220 1911.
Tues–Sat noon–5.30pm.
Small photographic gallery holding consistently interesting and well-presented exhibitions, often on local themes. Produces the lavish *Portfolio* magazine, in which the photos are accompanied by thoughtful essays and criticism.

Scottish Gallery

Map 4, F1. 16 Dundas St ⓒ558 1200.
Mon–Fri 10am–6pm, Sat 10am–4pm.
Blue-chip gallery in the New Town. Large space with shows of traditional and modern art, concentrating for the most part on better-known names.

Stills Gallery

Map 3, F2. 23 Cockburn St ⓒ225 9876.
Tues–Sat 11am–5pm.
Currently undergoing a major refurbishment, but still an important venue for photography. Features will include state-of-the-art darkrooms, studios and exhibitions.

GAY EDINBURGH

With an estimated homosexual population of around 15,000–20,000, Edinburgh has a dynamic **gay** culture which for years centred round the top of Leith Walk and Broughton Street, an area known as the "Broughton Triangle", where the first gay and lesbian centre appeared in the 1970s. The power of the Pink Pound has led to a proliferation of gay enterprises – some transitory, others more durable – and the rate of growth has quickened over the last few years.

The annual Gay Pride march takes place in June and alternates between Edinburgh and Glasgow, the next one scheduled for the capital in 1999. For further information on gay life in Edinburgh, check out *The List*, *Gay Scotland* (£1.85), a monthly publication, or *Scotsgay*, a bimonthly freesheet available in most pubs and clubs.

The important contact numbers are: Gay Men's Health (℗558 9444); Gay Switchboard (℗556 4049); Lesbian Line (℗557 0751). Solas 2 (℗661 0982) is an HIV and AIDS counselling service. Otherwise the best place for up-to-date information is at the Gay, Lesbian and Bisexual Centre which houses the *Stonewall Café* (see p.166).

CAFÉS

Blue Moon Café/Blue Moon Espresso

Map 4, J1. 1 Barony St & 36 Broughton St ☎557 0911.
Daily 7am–1am.

Two connected eating areas: the *Blue Moon Café*, with a
soothing fish tank and cool blue walls, is a great place to
meet, particularly relaxed during the day when a mixed
menu offers an all-day £4 breakfast and much else besides.
Soups, rolls and some hot dishes cooked in an American
and Mediterranean style. The *Blue Moon Espresso*, on the
main drag, is a smaller café offering snacks and drinks,
including an excellent cappuccino, for sitting in or taking
away.

Café Kudos

Map 2, H3. 22 Greenside Place ☎556 4349.
Daily: noon–1am.

Busy bar next to the Playhouse, attracting a crowd that is by no
means exclusively gay. Excellent vantage points on the first
floor for watching comings and goings within the bar and
outside. Good food available till 9pm and tables on the nice
wide pavement outside when the weather is good.

Over the Rainbow

Map 4, L1. 32c Broughton St ☎557 8969.
Mon–Sat noon–midnight. Closed Sun.

What with forests and a cute picket fence you'll have no
difficulty in working out which classic Hollywood movie
provided the inspiration for this suitably over-the-top yet
moderately priced bistro. Mainly pasta dishes, but plenty of
options for snacking.

Stonewall Café

Map 4, L1. 60 Broughton St ℂ478 7069.
Daily: April–Aug 11am–11pm; Sept–March noon–9.30pm.
Pleasant and bright licensed café at the back of Edinburgh's long-running Gay, Lesbian and Bisexual Centre, with a striking ceiling mural on the theme "We are one!". All-day breakfasts and light meals of soups and bacon rolls, along with snacks and coffees. Full of useful information on all aspects of gay life in Scotland's capital.

CLUBS AND BARS

CC Bloom's

Map 2, H3. 23 Greenside Place ℂ556 9331.
Mon–Fri 6pm–3am, Sat & Sun 3pm–3am. Free.
The only gay/lesbian bar in town to have a disco every night, playing nonstop, sweaty dance music from 10.30pm to 3am. Consistently Edinburgh's liveliest gay bar, with a friendly, welcoming crowd. Karaoke nights on Thursdays and Sundays, male dancers on Sunday afternoons.

French Connection

Map 4, C7. 89 Rose St Lane North ℂ226 7651.
Mon–Sat noon–1am, Sun 1pm–1am.
Well away from the rest of Edinburgh's gay bars and a much calmer atmosphere apart from karaoke nights on Tuesdays and Fridays. Small and cosy bar with a bunch of almost totally male friendly regulars looked after by the bar's owner, Babs.

Newtown Bar

Map 4, I2. 26 Dublin St ℂ538 7775.
Mon–Thurs noon–1am, Fri & Sat noon–2am; Sun 12.30pm–1am.
Still very near to the Broughton Triangle, but more of a New

Town feel to this smart, men-only bar, which attracts a high number of professionals. Downstairs, the aptly named Intense music night plays from Wednesday to Sunday.

Route 66

Map 2, H3. 6 Baxter's Place ⊘556 5991.
Mon–Fri 12.30pm–1am, Sat 12.30pm–12.30am, Sun 3pm–1am.
Another venue just down from the Playhouse, this is gay Edinburgh's closest thing to an ordinary pub. Entertainment nights include cabaret, live music and Saturday-night discos. Welcoming atmosphere and good real ale on tap. Cheap food served till 7pm.

SHOPS

PJ's

Map 4, L1. 60 Broughton St ⊘478 7069.
Mon–Sat noon–7pm, Sun noon–5pm.
At the front of the building housing the *Stonewall Café*, PJ's, whose slogan is "Ken and Barbie shop here, so should you", justifiably claims to be Scotland's largest gay and lesbian store. A range of clothing to start with, as well as numerous accessories including watches, magazines, cards and posters.

West and Wilde

Map 4, F1. 25a Dundas St ⊘556 0079.
Tues–Sat 10am–7pm, Sun noon–5pm. Closed Mon, except for June–Aug & Dec noon–5pm.
The only gay bookshop in town, this has a great selection of gay and lesbian literature and also stocks a handy array of gay paraphernalia: T-shirts, cards, videos and calendars. Mail order available.

KIDS' EDINBURGH

Older children will appreciate the historical wonders of Edinburgh covered in other parts of this book, especially the various castles. The 1pm gun in **Edinburgh Castle** is particularly fascinating to children, while there's a great soft play area within **Stirling Castle**. In the city centre, the **Royal Museum** on Chambers Street has a number of interactive displays as well as regular child-friendly lectures and is great for wet days.

The attractions we've listed below will appeal to younger children and any child interested in animals. **Edinburgh Zoo** and **Gorgie City Farm** offer contrasting choices of wild and tame animals, while the incredibly popular **Deep Sea World** is an imaginatively mounted display of all kinds of sea creatures, including conger eels and sharks. For entertainment of a more gentle kind, try **Edinburgh Butterfly and Insect World**.

Look out also for child-friendly events in the **Edinburgh International Science Festival** (☏557 4296) in April and the **Children's Festival** (☏554 6297) held the following month (see Festivals & Events for details). A separate programme, entitled *Festival for Kids*, is now published to give details of children's shows held during the Edinburgh Festival.

Deep Sea World

Map 1, B3. North Queensferry, Fife ✆01383 411411.
April–Oct daily 10am–6pm; Nov–March Mon–Fri 11am–5pm, Sat & Sun 10am–6pm; £5.80, children £3.50.

Hugely successful and already the second most visited attraction in Scotland, this is a well-thought-out mounted display of all kinds of sea creatures. The highlight, suitable for all but the youngest children, is a walk along a transparent acrylic tunnel surrounded by conger eels and sharks. Knowledgeable staff are on hand to allow the inquisitive to touch some of the gentler fish in the rockpool. The centre was involved in the attempted rescue of Moby, a whale that strayed up the Firth of Forth and eventually died on mud flats. The latest attraction is a piranha tank and there's a good café. The nearest railway station is North Queensferry. By car, cross the Forth Road Bridge, leave the M90 at Junction 1 and follow signs. At the busiest times, you will have to use a free park and-ride service operating from the road into North Queensferry.

Edinburgh Butterfly and Insect World

Map 1, F6. Melville Nursery, Lasswade, Midlothian ✆663 4932.
Daily 10am–5.30pm; £3.50.

Hundreds of brightly coloured butterflies and moths inside a large glasshouse. Streams and a bubbling mud pool add to the excitement, and at the back is a "Nocturnal World", with bee hives, scorpions, snakes and ants.

Edinburgh Zoo

Map 1, B4. Costorphine Rd ✆334 9171.
April–Sept Mon–Sat 9am–6pm, Sun 9.30am–6pm; Oct–March Mon–Sat 9am–4.30pm, Sun 9.30am–4.30pm; £6.

Edinburgh's zoo, two miles west of the city centre on the main Glasgow road, is well-served by a number of buses (#2, #26,

#31, #36, #69, #85, #86). Built on an 80-acre site stretching up the side of Costorphine Hill, with views across to the Pentlands, the zoo is best known for the penguin parade (daily March–Oct 2pm), which attracts large crowds; other delights for young children include polar bears, sea lions and several endangered species. A new evolution maze designed to show children the importance of water is great fun, though fastidious parents should be warned that few children emerge with their clothes dry.

Gorgie City Farm

Map 2, C9. 51 Gorgie Rd, Tynecastle Lane ℗337 4202.
Daily: March–Oct 9.30am–4.30pm; Nov–Feb 9.30am–4pm; free.
Lots of cute animals on a 2.5-acre site in the west of the city: sheep, hens, ducks and rabbits. An old tractor for clambering and a good picnic and play area. The adjacent *Farm Café* is well-prepared for children. Some organic produce for sale.

FOOD

The problems of taking young children out for a meal in Edinburgh are the same as anywhere in Britain, with many establishments unsuitable for children under the age of 10. The restaurants below have been chosen for their child-friendliness and the acceptable quality of the food for both adults and children. Apart from this selection, the **Royal Museum** on Chambers Street and the **National Gallery of Modern Art** both have child-friendly cafés.

Giuliano's

Map 1, E4. 1 Commercial St ℗554 5272.
Daily noon–10.30pm. Access, Diners and Visa. Moderate.
The big attraction here for children is to assemble their own pizzas and check out the electronic board displaying birthday messages.

There's also a good range of seafood dishes for those wanting something different.

Harry Ramsden's

Map 1, D4. 5 Newhaven Place ✆551 5566.
Daily noon–10pm. Access and Visa. Moderate.
Next door to the Newhaven fishing museum, this serves fish and chips and has a reasonable children's menu. There's a big play ship outside and a play area inside for rainy days.

Terrace Café

Map 2, C1. Royal Botanic Garden ✆552 0616.
Daily: April–Sept 10am–5pm; Oct–March 10am–2.30pm. Inexpensive.
Scones, cakes and juices, soup, baked spuds and coffee. The food's not stunning but the setting is. If you're lucky, the weather will be mild enough for you to be able to sit outside and enjoy the fantastic view across to the Old Town while the children gambol in the gardens.

Umberto's

Map 1, E4. 2 Bonnington Rd Lane ✆554 1014.
April–Sept daily noon–11pm; Oct–March Mon–Fri noon–2pm & 5–10pm, Sat & Sun noon–10.30pm. All cards. Moderate.
This is the best bet for anyone hoping to have a decent meal while the children are happy, with play areas both outside, in the enclosed garden, and inside, with trains and a wee house in the restaurant. Decent, realistic portions from about £2 for the young ones and a good choice starting from about £6 for a dish of pasta for anyone else.

KIDS' EDINBURGH: FOOD

SHOPPING

Despite the relentless advance of the big chains, central Edinburgh remains an enticing place for **shopping**, with many of its streets having their own distinctive character. **Princes Street** has been made pedestrian-friendly and, though dominated by standard chain outlets, retains a number of independent emporia, including at the eastern end the **Waverley Market**, a glossy mall of specialist and often expensive shops. The middle section of **Rose Street** has a good array of small jewellers and trendy clothes shops. Along the **Royal Mile** there are several distinctly offbeat places among the tacky souvenir sellers, and in and around **Grassmarket** you'll find arts and crafts shops plus some antiquarian booksellers. The main concentration of general, academic and remainder bookshops is in the area stretching from **South Bridge** to **George IV Bridge**. For antique shops, the two best areas are St Stephen Street in **Stockbridge** and **Causewayside** in Southside. Thursday night is late-night shopping, with many of the larger shops open till around 8pm.

Our listings are grouped into the following categories: books (p.173); clothes (p.175); music (p.177); food and drink (p.178).

BOOKS

Edinburgh's book scene is dominated by just two shops, the Scottish company James Thin and the national group Waterstone's, each with three well-stocked, efficiently run branches which are open late most nights. Check the individual shops and the local press for details of regular promotional readings. Edinburgh also has many secondhand bookshops, many of which are to be found in the Grassmarket area. Some of the best are listed below.

The Cooks' Bookshop

Map 3, D4. 118 West Bow ✆226 4445.
Mon–Fri 10am–5.30pm, Sat 10.30am–5.30pm.
Owned by Clarissa Dickson Wright, one of TV's "Two Fat Ladies", this bright shop has an attractive uncluttered display of books on every imaginable branch of cooking.

James Thin

53–59 South Bridge ✆556 6743 (Map 3, G3) & 57 George St ✆225 4495 (Map 4, C6).
Mon–Fri 9am–10pm, Sat 9am–5.30pm, Sun 11am–5pm.
One of Edinburgh's two best general bookstores, this is a long-established local institution. The South Bridge branch caters for University courses but has good sections of broader interest, with big travel and Scottish departments. The George Street branch covers most areas, including a handy selection of guides to modern technology, and has a famous old-fashioned café on the first floor.

McNaughtan's Bookshop

Map 2, H2. 3a–4a Haddington Place ✆556 5897.
Tues–Sat 9.30am–5.30pm.
Big shop at the top of Leith Walk, with all the main areas of the art

and literary world covered. Sections include history, travel, classics and an excellent choice of Scottish titles and antiquarian books. Searches undertaken for that elusive long-lost work. Not cheap.

Peter Bell

Map 3, B5. 68 West Port ℡229 0562.
Mon–Sat 10am–5pm.

Wide selection of quality secondhand books, concentrating on the academic end of the market. Philosophy, science, literature and history are all well-represented, with a healthy display of recent first editions.

Second Edition

Map 2, E1. 9 Howard Place ℡556 9403.
Mon–Fri noon–5.30pm, Sat 9.30–5.30pm.

A great location for an Edinburgh bookshop, opposite the house where Robert Louis Stevenson was born (8 Howard Place). It has a large collection of all sorts of secondhand books, said to number up to 20,000! The owner's choice of jazz makes this a pleasant place to while away an afternoon.

Waterstones

128 Princes St ℡226 2666 (Map 4, C8), 13–14 Princes St ℡556 3034 (Map 4, C8) & 83 George St ℡225 3436 (Map 4, C6).
Mon & Wed–Fri 9am–9pm, Tues 9.30am–9pm, Sat 9am–7.30pm, Sun 9am–7pm.

The customary tasteful Waterstone's recipe of browser-friendly shops. Particularly good for Scottish books, both fiction and non-fiction. Seattle Coffee Company have a café around the first-floor bay window of the 14 Princes Street branch (Mon–Thurs 9.30am–8pm; Fri & Sat 9.30am–7pm, Sun 11am–5pm) providing stupendous views across Princes Street Gardens to the castle.

Word Power

Map 2, H8. 43 West Nicolson St ℘662 9112.
Mon–Fri 10am–6pm, Sat 10.30am–6pm.
Small, well-laid-out radical book shop close to the University
with books on a number of interesting areas: feminist, gay and
lesbian, ecology, politics and black studies. Good general
literature section, with a healthy input from small independent
publishers.

For reviews of specialist gay bookshops, see p.167.

CLOTHES

Apart from the standard chain stores on Princes Street, the
St James Centre and the Gyle, outlets for Scottish specialities, such as tartans and woollens, can be found in the places
we've reviewed below. You should be able to find anything
from ball gowns to kitsch wear for that Seventies disco in
one of Edinburgh's many secondhand clothes shops, the
best of which are to be found in the Grassmarket/Cowgate
area.

Wm Armstrong

313 Cowgate ℘556 6521 (Map 3, G3) & 85 Grassmarket ℘220
5557 (Map 3, C4).
Mon–Fri 10am–5.30pm, Sat 10am–6pm, Sun noon–6pm.
The biggest of Edinburgh's second hand clothes shops selling a
vast range of garb, of both refined and dubious taste. Take your
pick from velvet or leather coats and jackets, denim shirts,
jackets and trousers, and just about any other style and cut of
the last fifty years.

Paddy Barrass

Map 3, C4. 15 Grassmarket ℡226 3087.
Mon–Fri noon–6pm, Sat 10.30am–5.30pm.
Small establishment selling vintage items. Clothing from the
Victorian and later eras including nightshirts, kilts and dinner
jackets. Also small linen and lace items, many of which are
displayed on the walls for inspection.

Byzantium

Map 3, E3. 9a Victoria St ℡225 1768.
Mon–Sat 10am–5.30pm.
Located in one of Edinburgh's many converted churches,
Byzantium has the air of a Sixties-style emporium with a
massive range of goods for sale under the one roof. Browse
through boutiques selling antiques, clothes from home and
abroad, books and prints, all of widely varying quality, before
going up to the airy mezzanine café, where a good vegetable
thali will cost you just £3.50.

Elaine's

Map 2, C3. 55 St Stephen St (no phone).
Mon–Sat 1–6pm.
From the sublime (Thirties ball gowns and cocktail dresses) to
the ridiculous (Seventies tank tops and flares) in one small
Stockbridge shop.

Geoffrey (Tailor)

Map 3, E8. 57–59 High St ℡557 0256.
Mon–Sat 9am–5.30pm, Sun 10am–5pm.
The place to go if you need to hire or buy a kilt. Highland
wear made on the premises for men and women. Various
Scottish gifts also on offer.

Jenners

Map 4, C8. 48 Princes St ℘225 2442.

Mon, Wed, Fri & Sat 9am–5.30pm, Tues 9.30am–5.30pm, Thurs 9am–7.30pm, closed Sun.

Edinburgh's most prestigious department store. Luxury items of every shape and size: a fantastic food hall and a sumptuous selection of toys, gifts and fashions.

MUSIC

For a wide range of mainstream music there are branches of the **Virgin Megastore** at 131 Princes St and **HMV** at 129 Princes St. For something more unusual, try one of the shops listed below.

Avalanche

17 West Nicolson St ℘668 2374 **(Map 2, H8) , 31a Dundas St** ℘556 0955 **(Map 4, F1) & 28 Lady Lawson St** ℘228 1939 **(Map 3, A5).**

Mon–Sat 10am–6pm, Sun (West Nicolson St only) noon–6pm.

Three busy shops traditionally specializing in indie stuff but nowadays also moving into the massive dance market. New and secondhand, with lots of bargains, especially in the West Nicolson St branch, for anyone prepared to spend some time digging around.

Backbeat

Map 2, H8. 31 East Crosscauseway ℘668 2666.

Mon–Sat 10am–5.30pm; Sun 12.30–5.30pm.

New and secondhand Southside shop with a huge choice in all formats. For many years, *Backbeat* has been strong on all forms of black music, with a particularly tasty selection of Northern Soul in the back room. Now also selling interesting rock records.

Bauermeister Records

Map 3, D9. 19 George IV Bridge ℭ226 5561.
Mon–Sat 9am–6pm.
Large selection of classical music tastefully presented and carefully tied in with visiting performers. Limited jazz and Scottish folk sections.

Vinyl Villains

Map 2, I3. 5 Elm Row ℭ558 1170.
Mon–Fri 10.15am–6pm, Sat 10.15am–5.30pm, Sun noon–4pm.
Sizeable secondhand store still stubbornly clinging on to a selection of secondhand records, but now moving with the times and selling CDs and all sorts of odd memorabilia. The choice is dominated by rock music, with a good range of old punk singles.

FOOD AND DRINK

On hot summer days, there are a number of places to pick up tasty sandwiches and snacks for an impromptu picnic in one of the city's many open spaces. Two premier addresses for souvenir hunters in search of Scotland's best-known specialities, haggis and whisky, are also given below.

Auld Alliance Bakery

Map 3, E3. 30 Victoria St ℭ622 7080.
Mon–Fri 8.30am–6pm, Sat 8.30am–5.30pm, Sun 10.30am–5pm.
Top-quality French baker, with a great selection of rustic

breads, both plain and with exotic flavours. Assorted sandwich fillings available, including smoked salmon, along with marinated olives and delicious cheese straws. Pastries and carrot cake for afters.

Lupe Pintos

Map 2, H9. 24 Leven St ℂ228 6241.
Mon–Sat 10am–7pm.
Fabulous shop offering Spanish and Mexican delicacies and mouth-stinging chilli with everything. Buy a sandwich filled with Spanish cheese or guacamole and some Mexican beer and chill out on Bruntsfield Links just round the corner. If you're really thirsty, there's always a big selection of bottles of tequila, with prices ranging from £13 to £35.

Charlie McNair's Deli and Sandwich Bar

Map 2, F8. 30 Forrest Rd ℂ226 6434.
Mon–Fri 9am–5.45pm, Sat 9am–4.30pm.
Small takeaway near the main hospital and the Meadows purveying great sandwiches and rolls with exotic flavours like spicy bean paté and delicious hummus. Wine, coffee and pastries also available. Big queues at lunchtime but always a pleasant atmosphere. Look out for Charlie in his other incarnation as a stalwart of the local jazz scene.

MacSween of Edinburgh

Map 2, H9. 118 Bruntsfield Place ℂ229 9141.
Tues–Fri 9.30am–5.30pm, Sat 9.30am–4.30pm. Closed Sun & Mon.
The best place to buy a haggis (Scotland's national dish) for an unsuspecting relative or friend. Something of an acquired taste, though undoubtedly worth sampling. You can even buy a

SHOPPING: FOOD AND DRINK

passable vegetarian version with kidney beans and lentils instead of meat.

Iain Mellis

Map 3, D3. 30 Victoria St ℗226 6215.
Mon–Sat 9.30am–6pm, Sun 9.30am–5.30pm.
A huge selection of delicious fresh cheese from all over Britain and Ireland, plus Italian Parmesan, the only foreign cheese they stock. The smells alone are wonderful, and the taste will make you swear off plastic supermarket cheese for ever.

Nature's Gate

Map 2, H9. 83 Clerk St ℗668 2067.
Mon–Sat 10am–7pm, Sun noon–4pm.
Vegetarian and vegan delights next to the Queen's Hall and close to the Meadows. Organic wines and beers, a big range of Japanese macrobiotic food and all sorts of goodies for anyone on a special diet, whether sugar- salt- or gluten-free. Plenty of choice also for lunches and snacks. *Isabel's* café in the basement serves similarly tasty food.

Real Foods

37 Broughton St ℗557 1911 (Map 4, L1) & 8 Brougham St ℗228 1201 (Map 2, D9).
Mon–Fri 9am–6pm, Sat 9am–5.30pm, Sun 11am–5pm.
The place to stock up on dried fruits, cereals, spices and a good selection of organic fruit and veg. For more immediate pleasures, sandwiches, snacks and all kinds of refreshing drinks are stored, including organic beers and wines. Also sells numerous health products. Don't miss the notice board for an insight into alternative Edinburgh.

Royal Mile Whiskies

Map 3, E8. 379–381 High St ©225 3383.
Mon–Sat 10am–6pm.
Solve all your present problems in this specialist shop opposite
St Giles, with everything the whisky enthusiast could ever
need. Recent and vintage malt and blended whisky in bottles
and miniatures. Smoked salmon and haggis also on offer.

Valvona and Crolla

Map 2, I3. 19 Elm Row ©556 6066.
Mon–Wed & Sat 8.30am–6pm, Thurs & Fri 8.30am–7pm.
The best Scottish Italian deli, now ninety years old, is full of
wallet-emptying Italian wonders: fresh bread, oozing cheeses,
pasta sauces and a huge selection of wine. The wonderful
choice has been further enhanced by the arrival of quality
vegetables, fresh from the Italian markets. Regular wine tastings
and cookery demonstrations.

FESTIVALS AND
EVENTS

The **Edinburgh Festival**, now the largest event of its kind in the world, first took place in 1947. For three weeks in August the atmosphere of Scotland's capital is transformed; the city centre is packed day and night through to the early hours. The Festival is made up of several strands, the original and grandest being the **International Festival**, a celebration of high-quality drama, dance and music. The **Fringe** grew alongside and quickly overtook the official Festival in terms of size: today it encompasses a huge range of expertise and organization. There are also concurrent **Film**, **Jazz** and **Book festivals**, leading to a feeling of culture overkill, with even the most ardent enthusiast able to sample only a minute fraction of what is on offer.

Aside from providing a substantial boost to the city's economy, the Festival does stage two events which regularly bring in huge crowds of townspeople: **Fringe Sunday**, when Holyrood Park is taken over for a vast open-air party, and the massive **firework display** and free concert, held in

Princes Street Gardens. And there are, of course, the annual Festival rituals: celebrity-spotting at the Assembly Rooms; newspaper gossip revolving around fears of imminent financial catastrophe for a major venue, if not the Festival itself; and the constant, raging debate about the strengths or otherwise of the Scottish element. Above all, though, there is a buzz to the city: the rumoured visit of a superstar, or even a soap star, the best and worst shows in towns, and the hot tips for the winners of the plethora of awards up for grabs, all become matters of supreme importance. By the Sunday following the end of the Festival, the performers have all departed: the winners to London for the various "Pick of the Fringe" seasons and the losers back home to dream of next year. The church halls and Masonic lodges are locked up, the traders and hoteliers count their takings and the city streets are quiet once again.

EDINBURGH INTERNATIONAL FESTIVAL

Driven by a desire for reconciliation and escape from post-war austerity, the Austrian Rudolf Bing, who was administrator of the Glyndebourne opera, brought together a host of distinguished musicians from the war-ravaged countries of central Europe for the **first Edinburgh Festival**. The symbolic centrepiece of his vision was the emotional reunion of Bruno Walter, a Jewish refugee from Nazi tyranny, and the Vienna Philharmonic Orchestra. At the same time, eight theatrical groups, both Scottish and English, turned up in Edinburgh, uninvited, performing in an unlikely variety of local venues, thus establishing the Fringe. Today more than a million people come to the city over three weeks (the last three in August, or the last fortnight and first week in September) to see several separate festivals, each offering a wide variety of artists and events –

everything is on show, from the highbrow to the controversial. However, the relationship between the official festival and the Fringe has become increasingly uneasy since the Fringe announced that, from 1998, it will begin and end a week earlier in order to coincide its final weekend with England's bank holiday.

....

The programme for the Edinburgh International Festival is available from April at 21 Market Street, EH1 1BW (©473 2000).

....

The legacy of Rudolf Bing's Glyndebourne connections ensured that, for many years, the official **Edinburgh International Festival** was dominated by opera. Although, in the 1980s, efforts were made to involve locals and provide a broader cultural mix of international theatre, dance and classical music, the official Festival is still very much a highbrow event.

Edinburgh International Film Festival

The **Film Festival** began at the same time as the main Festival, making it the longest-running film festival in the world. After a period in the doldrums, it has grown to its current position as a respected fixture on the international circuit, incorporating both mainstream and independent new releases and presenting a series of valuable retrospectives from Sam Fuller to Shohei Immamura. It also hosts interviews and discussions with film directors: in recent years' visitors have included Kenneth Anger, the Coen brothers, Clint Eastwood and Steve Martin. A particular feature has been the high-profile support given to Scottish film from Bill Douglas's austere and brilliant *Childhood* trilogy, through the lighter style of Bill Forsyth to the recent small-budget hit, *Shallow Grave*.

EDINBURGH INTERNATIONAL FILM FESTIVAL

> The Film Festival programme is published in early
> July: contact the Filmhouse, 88 Lothian Road, EH3
> 9BZ (©228 4051).

Fringe

For many years largely the domain of student revues – notable exceptions include Joan Littlewood's distinguished Theatre Workshop, with their early-1950s production of *The Other Animal*, about life in a concentration camp, and work by the great Spanish playwright, Lorca – the **Festival Fringe** began to really take off in the 1970s. Set up in 1951, the **Fringe Society** has grown from a small group to today's large-scale operation serving an annual influx of more than 500 acts – national theatre groups to student troupes – using around 200 venues. In spite of this expansion, the Fringe has remained loyal to the original open policy and there is still no vetting of performers. This means that the shows range from the inspired to the truly diabolical and ensures a highly competitive atmosphere, in which one bad review in a prominent publication means box-office disaster. Many unknowns rely on self-publicity, taking to the streets to perform highlights from their show, or pressing leaflets into the hands of every passer-by. Performances go on round the clock: if so inclined, you could sit through twenty shows in a day.

Over the years in both the official Festival and the Fringe, there has been a remarkable choice of both performers and venues: both Jean-Louis Barrault (star of 1945 movie *Les Enfants du Paradis*) and Richard Burton as Hamlet; Grace Kelly reading the works of early American poets; 65-year-old Marlene Dietrich in cabaret; *Macbeth* on Inchcolm Island in the Firth of Forth; and *2001: A Space Odyssey* performed to an audience sitting in a Hillman Avenger. The 1980s saw the anarchic circus performers Archaos, whose publicity involved sawing up cars outside the Fringe office. Although now disbanded, their spirit lives on in a number of ever more shocking shows, including a recent troupe of naked lesbian trapeze artists.

....

Contact the Festival Fringe Office, 180 High Street, EH1 1QS (©226 5257) for the Fringe programme that usually appears in June, and ring (©226 5138) for phone bookings from around the same time.

....

Book Festival

The **Book Festival**, which evolved from existing meet-the-author sessions to become an annual jamboree held in the douce setting of a marquee-covered Charlotte Square. Hundreds of established authors from throughout the English-speaking world come to take part in readings, lectures, panel discussions and audience question-and-answer sessions. For further information, contact the Scottish Book Centre, 137 Dundee Street, EH11 1BG (©228 5444).

Television Festival

The **Television Festival** is largely an in-house event, surfacing in the public consciousness only briefly as the keynote speaker indulges in the sport of deriding the latest changes at the BBC.

Jazz Festival

The **Jazz Festival** which has attracted the likes of Teddy Wilson and Benny Waters stages a lively parade through the Grassmarket (programme available in July from the office at 116 Canongate, EH8 8DD; ©557 1642).

Fireworks Concert

On the final Thursday of the Festival, a full orchestra in the Ross Bandstand in Princes Street Gardens plays pop classics accompanied by a spectacular fireworks display high up on the ramparts of the castle. Hundreds of thousands view from various vantage points throughout the city, the prime spots being Calton Hill or Inverleith Park in Stockbridge.

CALENDAR OF EVENTS

Quite apart from the August Festival, Edinburgh is now promoting itself as a year-round festival city, beginning the year with organized festivities for the Hogmanay period and continuing with assorted music and arts festivals throughout the year.

JANUARY/FEBRUARY/MARCH

Hogmanay
Edinburgh is gearing up to be the city to bring in the new millenium, with the **Hogmanay Festival** (℡557 3990) which involves a funfair on Waterloo Place at the east end of Princes Street, rock concerts and drive-in cinema shows. After building up steadily over a number of years, there has now been a big scaling-down following near-catastrophe in 1996 when overcrowding caused serious crushing at the foot of the Mound.

Rugby Internationals
Scotland's rugby union team plays home **internationals** every year on two winter Saturdays, against England, France, Wales or Ireland at Murrayfield Stadium in the west of the city.

Tickets for all games sell out extremely quickly; contact Scottish Rugby Union, 7-9 Roseburn Street (℡346 5000).

APRIL

Edinburgh International Science Festival
This festival (℡557 4296) incorporates hands-on children's events as well as numerous lectures on a vast array of subjects.

Folk Festival

The **Folk Festival** (℗556 3181) in April draws local and international performers.

MAY

Beltane Fire Festival

New Agey feel to this festival held on Calton Hill on the night of April 30 and May 1, the dominant images being fire-lighting and faces covered in woad. More conventionally, locals wash their faces in the dew on Arthur's Seat at dawn on May-Day.

Children's Festival

The **Children's Festival** (℗554 6297) is a large-scale annual event held in Inverleith Park in Stockbridge during the last week of May. Book readings, magic shows, mime and puppetry take place both inside a tented village and in the open air, while those who like to participate can go in for face painting and juggling lessons.

JUNE

Gay Film Festival

Celebration of **gay cinema** from around the world at the *Filmhouse* (℗228 2688).

Royal Highland Show

Vast agricultural fair held at Ingliston out near the airport. Yellow wellies and Range Rovers galore.

AUGUST

Edinburgh Military Tattoo

Although officially a separate event, the Edinburgh Military Tattoo, held in a splendid setting on the Castle Esplanade, is very much part of the Festival scene and an unashamed display of the kilt and bagpipes view of Scottish culture. Pipes and drums form the kernel of the programme, with a lone piper towards the end; performing animals, gymnastic and daredevil displays, plus at least one guest regiment from abroad, provide variety.

Although dubbed by many as elitist and irrelevant to locals, the Festival seems as much a part of the fabric of Edinburgh as its castle (one-third of the tickets are sold to local people).

Information and tickets are available from the Tattoo Office, 22 Market Street, EH1 1QB (℡225 1188).

SEPTEMBER

Open Doors Day

A great opportunity to visit a number of historically and architecturally interesting buildings, most of which are otherwise closed to the public. In recent years, these have included private homes in the New Town, disused churches and the marvellous Signet Library. Look out for leaflets in public buildings or contact the Cockburn Association (℡557 8686) for details.

FESTIVALS: CALENDAR OF EVENTS |

DIRECTORY

AIRLINES British Airways, 32 Frederick St (℃0345 222111). Other carriers handled by Servisair, Edinburgh Airport (℃344 3111).

BANKS Bank of Scotland, The Mound (head office), 38 St Andrew Square (℃442 7777); Barclays, 1 St Andrew Square (℃ 557 2733); Clydesdale, 29 George St (℃225 4081); Lloyds, 113–115 George St (℃226 4021); Midland, 76 Hanover St (℃ 456 3200); NatWest, 80 George St (℃226 6181); Royal Bank of Scotland, 42 St Andrew Square (head office: ℃556 8555); TSB, 120 George St (℃225 4555).

CAR RENTAL Avis, Europcar, Hertz and Alamo all run desks at Edinburgh Airport. Otherwise, try Arnold Clark, Lochrin Place (℃228 4747); Avis, 100 Dalry Rd (℃337 6363); Budget, 111 Glasgow Rd (℃334 7739); Carnies, 46 Westfield Rd (℃346 4155); Europcar, 24 East London St (℃557 3456); Hertz, Waverley Station (℃557 5272); Mitchells, 32 Torphichen St (℃229 5384); Thrifty Car Rental, 24 Haymarket Terrace (℃313 1613).

CONSULATES Australia, 25 Bernard St (℃467 8333); Belgium, 21 The Square, Penicuik (℃01968 679969); Canada,

3 George's St (✆0141 204 1373); Denmark, 4 Royal Terrace
(✆556 4263); France, 11 Randolph Crescent (✆225 7954);
Germany, 16 Eglinton Crescent (✆337 2323); Italy, 32
Melville St (✆226 3631); Netherlands, 53 George St (✆220
3226); Norway, 86 George St (✆226 5701); Spain, 63 North
Castle St (✆220 1843); Sweden, 6 St John's Place (✆554 6631);
Switzerland, 66 Hanover Place (✆226 5660); USA, 3 Regent
Terrace (✆556 8315).

EXCHANGE Thomas Cook, 79a Princes St (Mon–Fri
9am–5.30pm, Sat 9am–5pm, ✆220 4039). Outside normal
banking hours the best bet is to try one of the big city-centre
hotels, where you can expect a sizeable commission charge.

FOOTBALL Edinburgh has two Scottish Premier Division
teams, who play at home on alternate Saturdays during the
season which lasts from August to May. Heart of Midlothian
(or Hearts) play at Tynecastle Stadium, Georgie Rd, west of
Haymarket; Hibernian (or Hibs) play at Easter Road Stadium
in the east of the city. Both stadia are now all seater; tickets
from £10.

GENEALOGICAL RESEARCH Scots Ancestry Research
Society, 29a Albany St (✆556 4220); Scottish Genealogy
Society, 15 Victoria Terrace (✆220 3677); Scottish Roots,
57–59 High St (✆557 6550).

GOLF Apart from several prestigious private golf courses in
Edinburgh, there are also good public courses, the best being
the pair on the Braid Hills (✆447 6666). Others can be found
at Carrick Knowe, Balgreen Rd (✆337 1096), Craigentinny,
Craigentinny Ave (✆554 7501), Silverknowes, Silverknowes
Parkway (✆336 3843) and Portobello, Stanley St (nine-hole)
(✆669 4361).

HOSPITAL Twenty-four-hour casualty department at the Royal Infirmary, 1 Lauriston Place (©536 4000).

LAUNDRETTE Elm Row Automatic, 54 Elm Row (©556 4280); Canonmills laundrette, 7 Huntly St (©556 3199).

LEFT LUGGAGE Lockers available at Waverley Station (Mon–Sat 7am–11pm, Sun 8am–11pm) and St Andrew Square bus station (Mon–Sat 6.35am–10pm, Sun 8am–10pm).

LIBRARIES Central Library, George IV Bridge (Mon–Fri 9am–9pm, Sat 9am–1pm; ©225 5584). In addition to the usual departments, there's a separate Scottish section, plus an Edinburgh Room which is a mine of information on the city.

NEWSPAPERS The *Scotsman* is the city's quality daily paper with sound coverage of national and international news, and is strong on the arts. Its sister paper, the *Evening News*, covers local Edinburgh news, and the *Daily Record* is Scotland's most widely read tabloid.

PHARMACY Boots, 48 Shandwick Place (Mon–Sat 8am–9pm, Sun 10am–5pm; ©225 6757).

POLICE STATION In emergencies, phone ©999. For all other non-urgent enquiries, contact a local police station; Southside Police Station, Causeway ©667 3361; West End Police Station ©229 2323.

POST OFFICE 8–10 St James Centre (Mon 9am–5.30pm, Tues–Fri 8.30am–5.30pm, Sat 8.30am–6pm; ©0345 223344).

RAPE CRISIS CENTRE ©556 9437.

DIRECTORY

SPORTS STADIUM Meadowbank Sports Centre and Stadium, 139 London Rd (☎661 5351), is Edinburgh's venue for athletics events. The centre's facilities include an athletics track, a velodrome, and indoor halls offering a wide range of activities from badminton and squash to rock climbing and trampolining, many suitable for children.

SWIMMING POOLS The Royal Commonwealth Pool, 21 Dalkeith Rd (☎667 7211) has a modern 50m pool, a diving pool, a kid's pool and some great flumes. Elsewhere there are older public pools, some of which are very stylish: Caledonian Crescent (☎313 3964); Glenogle Rd (☎343 6376); 15 Bellfield St, Portobello (☎669 4077); 6 Thirlestane Rd (☎447 0052)

TRAVEL AGENTS Campus Travel (student and youth specialist), 53 Forrest Rd (☎225 6111) and 5 Nicolson Square (☎668 3303), Edinburgh Travel Centre (student and youth specialist), 196 Rose St (☎226 2019), 92 South Clerk St (☎667 9488), and 3 Bristo Square (☎668 2221).

CONTEXTS

History	197
Film	204
Books	206

History

Early settlement and the Middle Ages

The site of Edinburgh has been inhabited since the **Stone Age**; hunters and fishermen first came to the area around 5000 BC, to be followed two millennia later by farmers and shepherds. They in turn were succeeded by immigrant Beaker people from the continent, who introduced metalworking. In later periods of tribal warfare, forts were constructed on the extinct volcanic hills, notably **Castle Rock**, whose self-evident strategic value was of crucial importance in the subsequent rise of the city. This makes it seem all the more anomalous that the Romans, whose Imperial frontier lay just to the north, chose to build their fort close to the seashore at Cramond.

The name of Edinburgh – in its early forms of Dunedin or Din Eidyn ("Fort of Edin") – seems to have originated with the local tribes of the sixth century, rather than, as was long supposed, King Edwin of Northumbria, whose reign predated the **Northumbrian conquest** of the Lothians in 638 AD. Edinburgh subsequently remained under English control until the middle of the tenth century, when it was abandoned to the army of King Indulf of Scotland.

Castle Rock served as the nation's **southernmost border post** until 1018, when King Malcolm I's victory over the Northumbrians established the River Tweed as the permanent frontier with England. A half-century later, under King Malcolm III and St Margaret, who introduced Roman Catholicism to replace the indigenous Celtic church, the castle became one of the main seats of the Scottish court. It was probably also around this time that a town, which was immediately given the privileged status of a **royal burgh**, first began to grow up on the sloping ridge immediately to the east. In 1128 King David I established Holyrood Abbey at the foot of the slope, and shortly afterwards granted its monks permission to found a separate burgh, known as **Canongate**.

King Robert the Bruce granted Edinburgh a new charter in 1234, whereby the entire municipality, rather than its individual burgesses, was regarded as a vassal of the crown. He also gave it jurisdiction over the port of Leith, which was developed to take the place of the strategically vulnerable burgh of Berwick-upon-Tweed: the latter fell under English control four years later, and thereafter regularly passed backwards and forwards between the two countries. The prosperity brought by foreign trade enabled the newly fortified Edinburgh to establish itself as the undisputed capital of Scotland during the following century, with a fixed royal residence, central administration and law courts replacing the previous peripatetic setup.

Renaissance and Reformation

Under King James IV, the city enjoyed a short but brilliant **Renaissance era**. This saw not only the construction of a new residential palace alongside Holyrood Abbey, but also the granting of a royal charter to the College of Surgeons (the first of the city's long line of academic and professional bodies), and the establishment of the first printing press, which presaged an equally distinguished literary and publishing tradition.

This golden period came to an abrupt end in 1513 with the calamitous defeat by the English at the Battle of Flodden, which led to several decades of political instability. In the 1540s, King Henry VIII of England attempted to force a royal union ("the so-called Rough Wooing") with Scotland by having his son pledged in marriage to the infant Mary, Queen of Scots, which prompted the Scots to turn to France for help: French troops arrived to defend the city, while the young queen was despatched to Paris as the promised bride of the Dauphin.

Although the French occupiers succeeded in removing the English threat, they themselves antagonized the local citizenry, which had increasingly become sympathetic to the ideals of the **Reformation**. When the great preacher John Knox was allowed to return from exile in 1555, he became minister of Edinburgh's parish church, the High Kirk of St Giles, and quickly won the city over to his radical Calvinist message. A Protestant league, the Lords of the Congregation, appealed to Queen Elizabeth I of England for help, and in 1560 the French were driven out and Scotland proclaimed a Protestant nation.

The unions with England

Mary returned from France in 1561, but her fervent Catholicism was instrumental in dooming her reign to the status of a melodramatic interlude, and she was deposed in favour of her son, James VI. His rule saw the foundation of the **University of Edinburgh** in 1582 – giving Scotland its fourth institution of higher learning, a total England did not match until well into the nineteenth century. However, James's dynastic ambitions, resulting in his nomination as heir to the English throne, were to prove fateful for the city. Following the **Union of the Crowns** in 1603, it found itself totally upstaged by London: although the king promised to visit his northern capital every three years, it was not until 1617 that he made his one and only return trip.

In 1633 his son, Charles I, came to Edinburgh to be crowned, but soon afterwards precipitated a crisis by introducing episcopacy to the Church of Scotland, in the process making Edinburgh a bishopric for the first time in its history. Fifty years of religious turmoil followed, in which Catholicism made a spirited attempt at a comeback, before the ultimate triumph of **Presbyterianism**. Despite these vicissitudes, Edinburgh expanded throughout the seventeenth century, with a virtual tripling of its population to 57,000. In 1695, William Paterson, who had founded the Bank of England the previous year, set up the Bank of Scotland. This was to be the first major step in Edinburgh's development towards its present position as an international financial centre.

The **Union of the Parliaments** of 1707 dealt a further blow to Edinburgh's political prestige, though the guaranteed preservation of the national church, the distinctive legal and educational systems, and the special status of the royal burghs, ensured that it was never relegated to a purely provincial role.

The Enlightenment

Paradoxical as it may seem, it was in the second half of the eighteenth century that Edinburgh achieved the height of its influence, becoming a leading centre of the European **Enlightenment**. Internationally celebrated as, in the words of eighteenth-century novelist Tobias Smollett, "a hotbed of genius", it was home to a host of intellectual luminaries, including the philosopher and historian David Hume, the scientist James Hutton (founder of modern geology), and Adam Smith, father figure of the new discipline of political economy.

Inspired by the ideals of the Age of Reason, and under the leadership of a dynamic Lord Provost, George Drummond, the city belatedly began to expand beyond its cramped medieval boundaries. Following a public competition, a plan by James Craig was accepted in 1766 as the basis for the laying out of a **New Town** on a gridiron plan to the north of Castle Ridge. The result, one of the masterpieces of the European Neoclassical style, was so successful that separate northern, western and eastern extensions were made in the early nineteenth century.

Edinburgh's lofty intellectual reputation was maintained until well into the new century, and the city's greatest artist, Sir Henry Raeburn, immortalized the features of most of its leading figures in a magnificent series of portraits. The dominant figure of the era's last phase was the novelist and poet **Sir Walter Scott**, whose influence is almost impossible to exaggerate: his highly individual, extremely romantic vision of Scotland and its history inspired many of the greatest European writers, artists and composers of the nineteenth century, and (for good or ill) became implanted on popular imagination throughout the world.

The expansion of the city

Nineteenth-century **industrialization** affected Edinburgh less than any other major city in the British Isles, and it never lost its predominantly professional character. The industries which took a hold, such as brewing, distilling, confectionery and glass manufacturing, caused relatively little damage to the environment, and even the railway lines were concealed by the city's topography. Edinburgh lost its long-standing position as Scotland's largest city to Glasgow, which mushroomed into one of the industrial strongholds of the British Empire. Ever since then an intense rivalry has characterized relations between these two geographically close and mutually dependent (yet quite different) cities. Nonetheless, Edinburgh's status as capital was never threatened, and it became the automatic choice as head-quarters for the national institutions which began to be set up in the course of the century.

Though being outstripped by Glasgow, the city underwent an enormous **urban expansion** in the nineteenth century. The old burghs of Canongate, Calton and Portsburgh were incorporated into Edinburgh in 1856; the seaside resort of Portobello was added forty years later, and various new residential suburbs sprang up. In the meantime the Old Town, which had become notorious for its overcrowding and disease, was revitalized through the initiatives of the crusading conservationist and town planner, Patrick Geddes.

In 1920, the city boundaries were extended once again, reaching to Cramond in the west and the Pentland Hills in the south. Despite considerable local opposition, the port of Leith – which just over a century before had gained full municipal independence and thereafter developed into one of Scotland's largest towns – was annexed as well. Another important development was the **administrative devolution** granted just before World War II, whereby the Scottish Office was established in Edinburgh, replacing several UK ministries in the day-to-day running of the nation's internal affairs.

The postwar city

Edinburgh came through the war unscathed, and received another major fillip in 1947 when it was chosen as the permanent home for the great **International Festival** of music and drama which was established as a symbol of the new peaceful European order. Despite some hiccups, this has flourished ever since, in the process helping to make tourism one of the mainstays of the local economy. The

Fringe, originally set up as an adjunct to the main event, now ranks as the world's largest arts event in its own right, and several specialist festivals, which run concurrently, have likewise become established occasions.

Edinburgh has also been fortunate enough to escape the worst effects of the postwar **planning** policies which blighted so many British cities. There have been some unfortunate losses, notably much of George Square, which was torn down to make way for the tower blocks required by the fast-expanding University, and many fine shop fronts on the north side of Princes Street, sacrificed to chain-store uniformity. At the east end of the latter, the hideous St James Centre and New St Andrew House are blots on the magnificent cityscape, though things would have been much worse had plans for an inner-city ring road come to fruition. In 1975, Edinburgh carried out its latest territorial expansion, moving its boundaries westwards as far as the old burgh of South Queensferry and the Forth Bridges.

Four years later, with Scottish Nationalism in the ascendant, the Labour government proposed a scheme for **political devolution**, whereby the activities of the Scottish Office would be subject to an elected assembly in Edinburgh. This was put to a referendum, but, although the scheme narrowly won a majority of votes cast, it failed to gain the required support of 40 percent of the electorate. The Conservative government which took office later the same year was implacably opposed to the idea of devolution — a hardline stance which eventually had the reverse of its desired effect. As the Tories kept winning election after election in England, so their support in Scotland dwindled, and the opposition parties became united in their determination to introduce some form of home rule. In May 1997, Edinburgh, along with the rest of Scotland, voted out its remaining Conservative MPs, and in the referendum held in September of the same year there was a large majority in favour of the Labour government's proposal to establish a parliament in Edinburgh with tax-raising powers. As a result, Scotland's capital is due to enter the new millennium as a centre of political power once more.

Film

In spite of the city's photogenic qualities, surprisingly few films have been made entirely in Edinburgh. The city has been used more often to provide an elegant setting for isolated scenes: the *Café Royal* and Arthur's Seat were used in the Oscar-winning *Chariots of Fire*; the 1995 film *Jude* featured Parliament Square, used in place of the too-modern-looking Oxford; and the Royal Mile appeared in *Mary Reilly*, a disastrous version of *Jekyll & Hyde* starring John Malkovich and Julia Roberts. The huge success of *Trainspotting,* however, may lead to a greater number of Edinburgh-made films in the future – indeed, work on other stories by Irvine Welsh is already under way. The following are the pick of the movies with an Edinburgh setting.

Waverley Steps (John Eldridge, 1947). A hangover from World War II propaganda, this "Lets-all-get-on-together" documentary shows postwar life in the capital, social differences and all, through the eyes of a visiting Danish sailor.

Happy Go Lovely (Bruce Humberstone, 1950). Millionaire David Niven and chorus girl Vera Ellen get together during the Edinburgh Festival.

Battle of the Sexes (Charles Crichton, 1959). Ealing-style comedy, based on a short story by James Thurber, in which a mild-mannered Peter Sellers seeks to disrupt an efficiency drive at an Edinburgh tweed factory led by Constance Cummings.

Greyfriars Bobby (Don Chaffey, 1960). No prizes for guessing which American company, well-known for classic anthropomorphic cartoons, made this version of Edinburgh's most sentimental tale, previously filmed in 1949 as *Challenge to Lassie*. Although there were too many TV aerials in the environs of Greyfriars Kirk to allow filming, local actors were used, including Donald Crisp as the dog's owner and Andrew Cruickshank as the city's Lord Provost.

The Prime of Miss Jean Brodie (Ronald Neame, 1969). Maggie Smith won an Oscar for her portrayal of the eccentric teacher in this well-regarded version of Muriel Spark's classic tale of life in an Edinburgh girls' school.

My Childhood, **My Ain Folk** and **My Way Home** (Bill Douglas, 1972–78). Powerful, moving and unremittingly bleak trilogy of films on growing up in the mining town of Newcraighall, on the eastern tip of the city. Sadly, Douglas died in 1991 never having filmed his screenplay of James Hogg's *Confessions of a Justified Sinner*.

Restless Natives (Michael Hoffman, 1985). Comic tale of a couple of young lads from an Edinburgh housing scheme who hold up American tourists and become celebrities.

Tickets to the Zoo (Brian Crumlish, 1994). A look at the problems caused by youth unemployment in the Eighties, set in Costorphine and Leith.

Shallow Grave (Danny Boyle, 1995). Three Edinburgh yuppies get lucky then squabble over the proceeds in a patchy film noir. The exciting opening sequence shows a car racing through the New Town.

Trainspotting (Danny Boyle, 1996). This hugely successful film version of Irvine Welsh's best-selling novel of Edinburgh lowlife kicks off with a great chase along Princes Street.

FILM

Books

Many of the books listed below are in print and in paper-back – those that are out of print (o/p) should be easy to track down in secondhand bookshops. Publishers follow each title; first the UK publisher, then the US. Only one publisher is listed if the UK and US publishers are the same. Where books are published in only one of these countries, UK or US comes after the publisher's name.

Fiction

Iain Banks, *Complicity* (Abacus; Bantam). Typically lurid tale by Scotland's best contemporary author, dealing with a journalist on *The Caledonian* (a barely disguised *Scotsman*) himself caught up in paranoia and misdeeds.

Pat Barker, *Regeneration* (Penguin; Nal-Dutton). First part of the prizewinning trilogy based on the real-life meeting of Siegfried Sassoon and Wilfred Owen in Edinburgh's Craiglockhart Hospital, where the two try to come to terms with the horrors they have witnessed in the trenches.

Christopher Brookmyre, *Quite Ugly One Morning* (Abacus, UK). Cynical investigative journalist, Jack Parlabane, sorts out skullduggery in an Edinburgh NHS trust hospital in a hard-boiled post-Irvine Welsh novel.

James Hogg, *Confessions of a Justified Sinner* (Penguin). Scary tale, first published in 1824, of the inner torments of the human psyche; an inspiration for much later Scottish fiction.

Paul Johnston, *Body Politic* (New English Library, UK). Blues fanatic private investigator Quentin Dalrymple handles a series of grisly murders in the brave new world of 2020 AD when Edinburgh, the only stable city in the British Isles, exists largely to serve a massive tourist industry.

Eric Linklater, *Magnus Merriman* (Canongate). Vivid descriptions of Edinburgh landmarks in this humorous

satire of the Scottish literary and political world of the
1930s.

Ian Rankin, *Knots and Crosses* (Coronet o/p; St Martin's
Press), *Hide and Seek* (Coronet o/p; Simon & Schuster) Jazz-
loving copper John Rebus trawls through Edinburgh lowlife.

Sir Walter Scott, *The Waverley Novels* (Penguin). The books
that did much to create the romanticized version of Scottish
life and history.

Robert Louis Stevenson, *The Scottish Stories and Essays*
(Edinburgh University Press); *Dr Jekyll & Mr Hyde* (Penguin).
The former includes "The Misadventures of John Nicholson",
an entertaining account of an innocent's escapades, and the
grisly "The Body Snatchers". Though nominally set in London,
Stevenson's classic, and still resonant, horror story of Jekyll
and Hyde is generally considered to be based on the author's
misspent youth in the bowels of Edinburgh's Old Town.

Irvine Welsh, *Trainspotting* (Minerva; Heinemann). No-holds-barred
account of Nineties Edinburgh lowlife; sordid and guttural.
Marabou Stork Nightmares (Vintage; Norton) is similarly gross but
has more of a plot. *Ecstasy* (Vintage; Norton), a collection of three
novellas published in 1996 at the height of *Trainspotting* fever,
covered the same ground and suggested either a rushed job or
that Welsh was beginning to run out of ideas.

History

Robert Chambers, *Traditions of Edinburgh 1824* (Chambers).
An extraordinary collection of lively tales, many of which
would today count as urban myths, about the Old Town
streets and closes.

David Daiches, *Two Worlds* (Canongate, UK); *Edinburgh*
(Constable, UK). The first is a very dry account of growing up
in Edinburgh in the 1920s as the son of the city's chief rabbi.
Glimpses of a lost world with its own hybrid language,
Scottish Yiddish, now long vanished. A single-volume history

full of entertaining material, *Edinburgh* is especially strong on the city's literary history.

Michael Lynch, *Scotland: A New History* (Pimlico, UK). Acclaimed recent history of Scotland.

Charles McKean, *Edinburgh: Portrait of a City* (Century o/p, UK); A short, elegantly written account of the city's history.

Eileen Miller, *The Edinburgh International Festival 1947–1996*. (Scolar Press). Dry account of the history of the Festival; includes cast lists for every major production over the period.

Sandy Mullay, *The Edinburgh Encyclopedia* (Mainstream, UK). For the completist, a huge amount of detail about every corner of Edinburgh's history, from the colours of school rugby shirts to listings of all the city's MPs.

Art and architecture

John Gifford, Colin McWilliam and David Walker, *The Buildings of Scotland: Edinburgh* (Penguin, UK). Scholarly architectural account of the city's buildings. Critical where necessary, but full of praise for the great monuments of the Old and New Towns.

Charles McKean, *Edinburgh: An Illustrated Architectural Guide* (RIAS Publications). A beautifully produced, slim guide to Edinburgh's buildings, full of pertinent and judicious comments and quotations.

Duncan Macmillan, *Scottish Art 1460-1990* (Mainstream). Authoritative and up-to-date guide through the history of Scottish art with all the big names receiving due attention.

Robert Louis Stevenson, *Edinburgh: Picturesque Notes* (Barnes & Noble). This collection of beautifully-crafted vignettes couched in hyper-refined prose is considered by most experts to be the finest book ever written about Edinburgh.

A.J. Youngson, *The Making of Classical Edinburgh* (Edinburgh University Press; Colorado University Press). Full account, with wonderful illustrations, of the creation of the New Town.

INDEX

A

Abbey Lairds 38
Abbey Strand 38
accommodation 97–110
Ainslie Place 70
airlines 190
airport 5
Anchor Close 30
Ann Street 71
Arthur's Seat 42
Assembly Hall 20

B

banks 190
bars (see pubs)
Bible Land 33
books 206–208
Brass Rubbing Centre 31
Brodie's Close 22
Brodie, William 23
bus terminal 5

C

Calton 74
Calton Hill 74
Calton Jail 74
campsites 109
campus accommodation 106
Cannonball House 10
Canongate 33
Canongate Kirk 35
Canongate Tolbooth 33
car rental 190
Castlehill 18
Chalmer's Close 31
Charlotte Square 66
Chessel's Court 33

child-friendly restaurants 170–171
childrens' activities 168–170
cinemas 159–160
City Chambers 29
City Observatory 75
classical music 152
clubs 152–155
consulates 190
Covenanters 50
Cowgate 46
Craigmillar Castle 44
Cramond 80
Crichton Castle 91
Croft an Righ 39
cycle paths 8

D

Dalmeny House 79
Deacon Brodie 23
Dean Bridge 70
Dean Village 71
Dirleton Castle 90
Duddingston 43
Duddingston Kirk 43
Dugald Stewart Monument 75

E

Edinburgh Castle 9–17
Edinburgh Experience 75
Edinburgh Old Town Weaving Centre 20
exchange (money) 191

F

Festival, Edinburgh
    International 183–184
festivals 182–189
film 204–205
Film Festival 184

Flodden Wall 51
football 191
Forth Rail Bridge 77
Forth Road Bridge 77
Fringe 185–186

G

galleries 161–163
gay bars 166–167
gay cafés 165–166
gay clubs 166–167
gay information 164
gay shops 167
Geddes, Patrick 19
genealogical research 191
George Heriot's Hospital 51
George IV Bridge 48
George Street 66
Georgian House 67
Gladstone's Land 21
golf 191
Goose-Pie House 19
Grassmarket 48
Greyfriars Bobby 49
Greyfriars Kirk 51
Greyfriars Kirkyard 49
guesthouses 102–106

H

Heart of Midlothian 25
High Kirk of St Giles 25
High Street 27
history of Edinburgh 197–204
Hogmanay 187
Holyrood Abbey 41
Holyrood Park 42
Holyroodhouse 39–41
Hopetoun House 77
hospitals 192
hostels 107–109
hotels 98–102
Huntly House 36

I

Inchcolm Abbey 79

J

James Court 21
John Knox's House 32
Knox, John 32, 34
Lady Stair's House 22
laundries 192
Lauriston Castle 81
Law Courts 24
Lawnmarket 21
left luggage 192
Leith 81–83
libraries 192
Linlithgow Palace 87

M

MacMorran's Close 22
Magdalen Chapel 47
Mansfield Place Church 70
Marlin's Wynd 30
Mary King's Close 29
Mercat Cross 25
Military Tattoo 188–189
Milne's Court 21
Monument to Dugald Stewart 75
Moray Place 70
Mound, the 59
Museum of Childhood 31
music venues 150–152

N

National Gallery of Scotland ... 60–66
National Library of Scotland 48
National Monument 75
Nelson Monument 75
New Town 55–75
Newhaven 83
newspapers 192
North British Hotel 58

O

Old Calton Burial Ground 74
Old College 53
Old Observatory 75
Old Royal High School 74
Old Town Information Centre 30

Outlook Tower 20

P

Paisley Close 30
Palace of Holyroodhouse 39–41
Danmure House 36
Parliament House 24
Parliament Square 23
People's Story 35
pharmacy 192
police 192
Portobello 84
post office 192
Princes Street 56–60
pubs 139–148
    Leith 146
    New Town 143–145
    Newhaven 147
    Old Town 140–143
    Southside 146
    suburbs 148
    Tollcross 146

Q

Queen Mary's Bath House 38
Queen Street 67

R

Ramsay Gardens 18
Randolph Crescent 70
rape crisis centre 192
Register House 57
restaurants 111–138
    Leith: brasseries and cafés 129
        Chinese 130
        Fish and seafood 130
        Indian 131
        Italian 132
        Scottish 132
    Lothian Road and Tollcross: brasseries
    and cafés 136
        Chinese 137
        French 137
        Indian 138
        Scottish 138

New Town: brasseries and cafés 120
    American 121
    Chinese 122
    French 122
    Fish and seafood 123
    Indian 124
    Italian 124
    Mexican 125
    Moroccan 125
    Scottish 126
    Southeast Asia 127
    Spanish 128
    Vegetarian 128
Old Town: brasseries and cafés 112
    French 115
    Indian 116
    Italian 117
    Scottish 117
    Spanish 118
    Vegetarian 119
Southside: brasseries and cafés 132
    Chinese 133
    French 133
    Indian 134
    Mexican 135
    North African 135
    Scottish 135
    Vegetarian 136
Riddle's Court 22
Rosslyn Chapel 92–94
Royal Botanic Garden 73
Royal Mile 18–36
Royal Museum of Scotland 52
Royal Scottish Academy 59

S

St Andrew's church 66
St Andrew's House 74
St Andrew's Square 66
St Bernard's Well 71
St Cecilia's Hall 46
St Cuthbert's Kirk (Lliameny) 80
St James Centre 57
Scotch Whisky Heritage Centre 19
Scott Monument 58
Scottish National Gallery
    of Modern Art 71–73

Scottish National Portrait Gallery 68
Shoemaker's Land 33
shops 172–181
sightseeing tours 7
Signet Library 24
South Queensferry 77
sports stadium 193
Stevenson, Robert Louis 28
Stirling Castle 88–90
Stockbridge 71
swimming pools 193

T

Talbot Rice Art Gallery 54
Tantallon Castle 91
taxis 7
theatres 157–159
Tolbooth Kirk 20

tourist office 5
travel agents 193
travel passes 6
Trinity Apse 31
Tron Kirk 30

U

University of Edinburgh 53

W

Water of Leith 70
Waterloo Place 74
Waverley Market 58
Waverley Station 5
West Bow 48
West Register House 66
Whitehorse Close 36

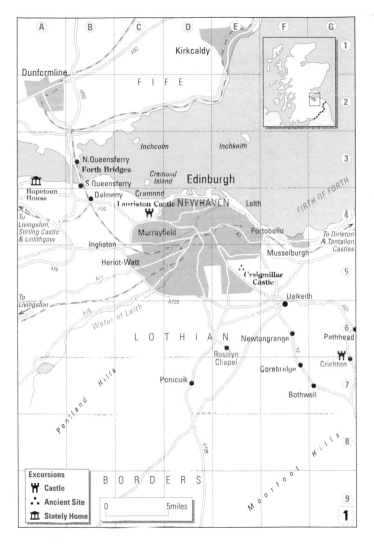

Excursions

🏰 Castle
∴ Ancient Site
🏛 Stately Home

0   5miles

1

Kirkcaldy

Dunfermline

F I F E

Inchcolm   Inchkeith

N.Queensferry
Forth Bridges

Cramond
Island   Edinburgh

S.Queensferry

🏛 Hopetoun House

Dalmeny

Cramond

Lauriston Castle NEWHAVEN   Leith

FIRTH OF FORTH

To Livingston, Stirling Castle & Linlithgow

Murrayfield

Portobello

Ingliston

To Dirleton & Tantallon Castles

Heriot-Watt

Musselburgh

Craigmillar Castle

To Livingston

Water of Leith

Dalkeith

L O T H I A N   Newtongrange

Pathhead

Rosslyn Chapel

Gorebridge

Crichton

Penicuik

P e n t l a n d   H i l l s

Bothwell

M o o r f o o t   H i l l s

B O R D E R S

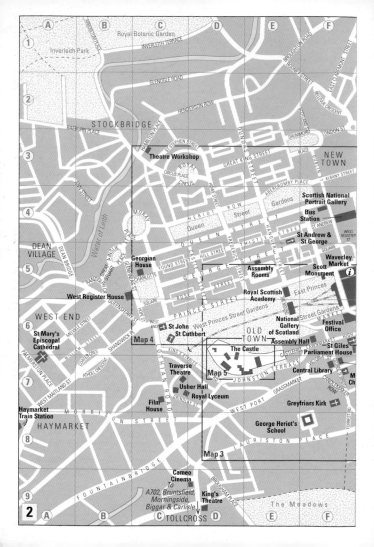

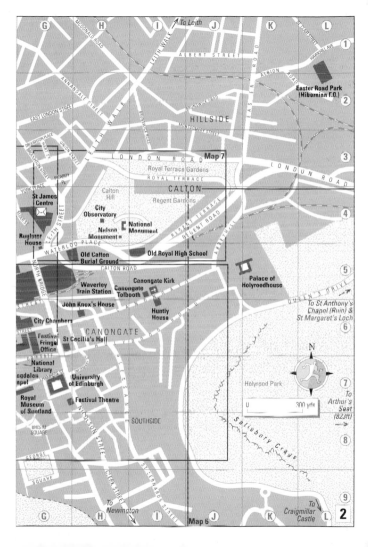

To Leith

ALBERT STREET

G

H

I

J

K

L

MCDONALD ROAD

ANNANDALE STREET

LEITH WALK

EAST LONDON STREET

BRUNSWICK ROAD

MONTGOMERY STREET

HILLSIDE

EASTER ROAD

SCIENNAR STREET

HIGHHILL AVE

Easter Road Park
(Hibernian F.C.)

DUBLIN STREET

YORK PLACE

FORREST

BROUGHTON STREET

DR ASHTON PLACE

BROUGHTON PLACE

DR APUT

UNION STREET

ELM STREET

LONDON ROAD **Map 7**

LONDON ROAD

Royal Terrace Gardens

ROYAL TERRACE

St James
Centre

City
Observatory

Calton
Hill

CALTON

Regent Gardens

Register
House

Nelson
Monument

National
Monument

REGENT TERRACE

REGENT ROAD

WATERLOO PLACE

ELM STREET

CALTON ROAD

Old Calton
Burial Ground

Old Royal High School

ARSENAL

NORTH BRIDGE

Waverley Train Station

Canongate Kirk

Canongate
Tolbooth

Palace of
Holyroodhouse

QUEEN'S DRIVE

John Knox's House

Huntly
House

To St Anthony's
Chapel (Ruin) &
St Margaret's Loch

City Chambers

Festival Fringe
Office

St Cecilia's Hall

CANONGATE

JEFFREY STREET

National
Library

Magdalen
Chapel

University
of Edinburgh

Royal
Museum
of Scotland

Festival Theatre

N

Holyrood Park

300 yds

BRISTO
SQUARE

NICOLSON STREET

SOUTHSIDE

ST LEONARDS STREET

To
Arthur's
Seat
(823ft)

Salisbury Crags

GEORGE
SQUARE

CHAPEL STREET

BUCCLEUCH STREET

To
Newington

Map 6

G

H

I

J

K

L

To
Craigmillar
Castle

1

2

3

4

5

6

7

8

9

2

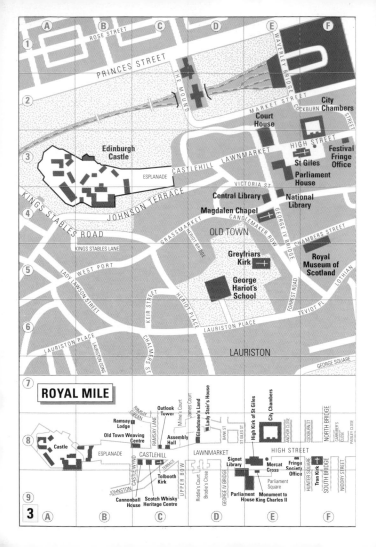

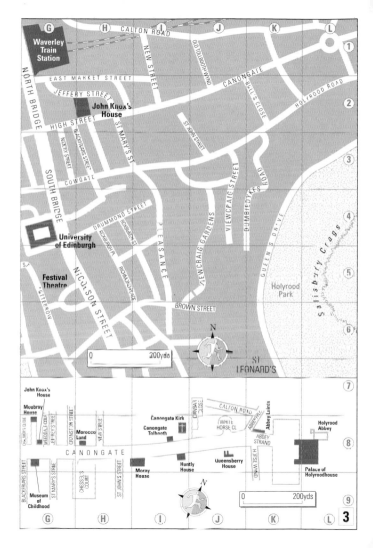

Top map labels:

Waverley Train Station

CALTON ROAD

NEW STREET

OLD TOLBOOTH WYND

CANONGATE

HOLYROOD ROAD

EAST MARKET STREET

JEFFERY STREET

John Knox's House

ST MARY'S ST

ST JOHN STREET

BAILIE'S CLOSE

NORTH BRIDGE

HIGH STREET

BLACKFRIARS STREET

NIDDRY STREET

COWGATE

ST ASAPH STREET

VIEWCRAIG STREET

DUMBIEDYKES ROAD

SOUTH BRIDGE

DRUMMOND STREET

SCHOOLYARD

ROXBURGH ST

PLEASANCE

VIEWCRAIG GARDENS

QUEEN'S DRIVE

University of Edinburgh

Salisbury Crags

Festival Theatre

NICOLSON STREET

RICHMOND PLACE

BROWN STREET

Holyrood Park

GIFFERROW

N

0   200yds

ST LEONARD'S

Bottom map labels:

John Knox's House

Moubray House

Canongate Kirk

CALTON ROAD

DUNBAR'S CLOSE

WHITE HORSE CL.

Abbey Lairds

Holyrood Abbey

JEFFREY'S STREET

TWEEDDALE COURT

CRANSTON STREET

NEW STREET

Morocco Land

Canongate Tolbooth

ABBEYHILL

ABBEY STRAND

CANONGATE

BLACKFRIARS STREET

ST MARY'S STREET

CHESSEL'S COURT

ST JOHN'S STREET

Moray House

Huntly House

Queensberry House

DUMBIEDSKH

Palace of Holyroodhouse

Museum of Childhood

N

0   200yds

3

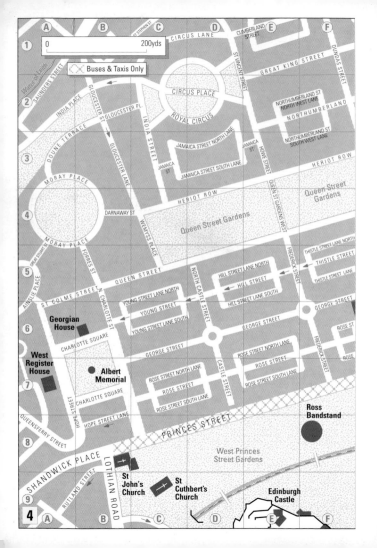

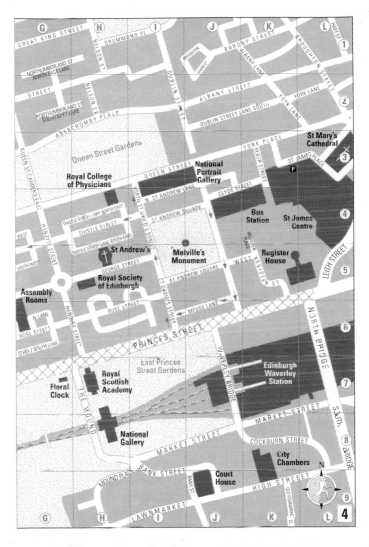

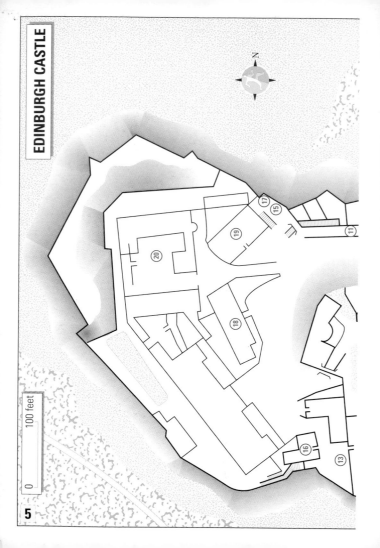

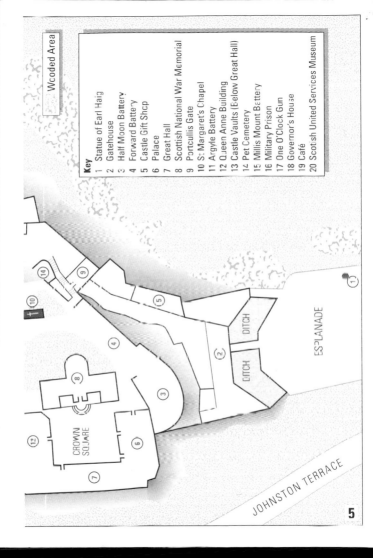

Wooded Area

Key
1 Statue of Earl Haig
2 Gatehouse
3 Half Moon Battery
4 Forward Battery
5 Castle Gift Shop
6 Palace
7 Great Hall
8 Scottish National War Memorial
9 Portcullis Gate
10 St Margaret's Chapel
11 Argyle Battery
12 Queen Anne Building
13 Castle Vaults (Below Great Hall)
14 Pet Cemetery
15 Mills Mount Battery
16 Military Prison
17 One O'Clock Gun
18 Governor's House
19 Café
20 Scottish United Services Museum

CROWN
SQUARE

DITCH

DITCH

ESPLANADE

JOHNSTON TERRACE

5

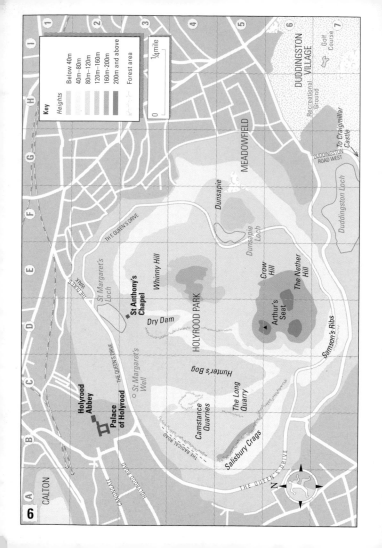

Key

Heights
- Below 40m
- 40m–80m
- 80m–120m
- 120m–160m
- 160m–200m
- 200m and above
- Forest area

0 ¼mile

CALTON

Holyrood Abbey

Palace of Holyrood

THE QUEEN'S DRIVE

THE QUEEN'S DRIVE

St Margaret's Well

St Margaret's Loch

RADICAL ROAD

THE PRINCE'S WALK

THE RADICAL ROAD

Camstance Quarries

Salisbury Crags

Hunter's Bog

The Long Quarry

St Anthony's Chapel

Whinny Hill

Dry Dam

HOLYROOD PARK

Samson's Ribs

Arthur's Seat

Crow Hill

The Nether Hill

Dunsapie

Dunsapie Loch

MEADOWFIELD

DUDDINGSTON ROAD WEST

To Craigmillar Castle

Duddingston Loch

DUDDINGSTON VILLAGE

Golf Course

Recreational Ground

N

THE QUEEN'S DRIVE

6